CW00519535

Steep Holm
AT WAR
RODNEY LEGG

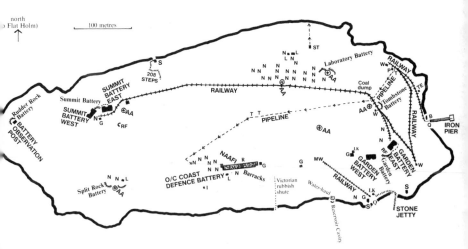

north
(to Flat Holm)

100 metres

MAP: the island as part of the
MIXED DEFENCES SEVERN

Upper and lower case lettering =
Palmerstonian fortifications, 1866-68
Stippled features = Palmerstonian buildings

CAPITAL LETTERS = Second World War fortifications, 1941
Solid features = Second World War buildings

KEY:

AA	= Anti-Aircraft gun	**L**	= Latrines	**P**	= Pump house	**R**	= Reservoir
B	= Boathouse	**LK**	= Limekiln	**PW**	= Power winch	**RF**	= Range finder
G	= Generator house	**MW**	= Manual winch	**Q**	= Quay (1866)	**ST**	= Sewage tank
I	= Incinerator	**N**	= Nissen hut	**Q**	= Quay (1941)	**T**	= Water tank

TE = Telephone exchange
W = Winch house

WINCANTON PRESS NATIONAL SCHOOL NORTH STREET
WINCANTON SOMERSET BA9 9AT

To Frank Harris,
who discovered Steep Holm
through 'True Tilda'.

First published 1991. Copyright Rodney Legg © 1991. Usual rights reserved though extracts may be used without further permission provided the source is acknowledged and the work of the Kenneth Allsop Memorial Trust, in conserving Steep Holm island, is mentioned. For other requests consult Rodney Legg on 0963 32583.

Typeset by Reg Ward at Holwell, Dorset, and output by Wordstream Limited at Poole. Photographic bromides by Flaydermouse (sic) Printing Studio, Yeovil, and layout by Rodney Legg.

Printed in Great Britain, with assistance from Adrian Ollerton, by Printhaus Graphique Limited (a Euroname!) of Round Spinney, Northampton. Distribution by Maurice Hann of 36 Langdon Road, Parkstone, Poole, Dorset BH13 9EH (telephone 0202 738248).

ISBN (International Standard Book Number) 0 948699 60 4

Contents

OPPOSITE – Amanda Allsop, daughter of broadcaster Kenneth Allsop in whose memory Steep Holm was purchased: beside Victorian gun barrel No 72 in Laboratory Battery West. Seen from the south. Photographed by Rodney Legg in 1973.

Garden Battery East: Cardiff scrap merchant 'F. SMALL' left his name etched large on this gun barrel from the western of the two Palmerstonian barbettes of 1866-68. He failed to cut-up the Garden Battery cannon in 1903 (though this has a deep incision to show he tried; as he did its eastern partner which is now lost). Seen from the north-west; with Salman Legg. Photographed by Rodney Legg in 1991.

Introduction
– to the Steep Holm trilogy:
the first book is *Steep Holm Legends and History,*
and the third *Steep Holm – Allsop Island*

You can find Britain in microcosm on an offshore island. That has to be the justification for inflicting a quarter of a million words on what is barely fifty acres of rock. Thomas Hardy, who had less need of excuses, felt it better to know a small area exceedingly well than the whole of the world a little.

Steep Holm is poised on the horizon between England and Wales, half-way between Weston-super-Mare and Cardiff at latitude 51 degrees 20½ minutes north, longitude 3 degrees 6½ minutes west; the next place in the latter direction is Goose Cove, Newfoundland. The island has been touched by events from both sides of the Bristol Channel. Occupants have included the Romans, the Danes, the Christians, the Coast Guard and the Royal Artillery.

None found it tractable. This is nature's environment. Botanical explorers may come on tropical days and find their flowers but otherwise the island maintains hostility to man. It performs better when left to the seabirds but even they never find peace.

I have been asked to point out that the views expressed, particularly in the third book, are often my own rather than those of the Allsop Trust's current council. My response is that this is an investigation into contemporary history and the opinions belong where they are attributed. Many were indeed those of the Trust as an organisation, or its officers, at the time they were expressed. Subsequent adjustment and revision is not, fortunately, a problem for the historian. As L.P. Hartley writes in *The Go-Between*: "The past is another country, they do things differently there."

Truth, I feel upon a reminder from Michael Yardley, is the only god an historian serves – though how well is open to doubt as I have deleted three substantial references in the face of sensitivity from others.

I have not, however, agreed to the removal of the quotations from "private correspondence never intended for publication" as none of it was secret at the time. With few exceptions, and those where quoted here are hurtful to me rather than to others, such extracts have been read to meetings of the Kenneth Allsop Memorial Trust or otherwise reported to its officers and in some cases even circulated to the press. "This could destroy all faith in your integrity," I have been told. If so, I shall be the loser, but what you have here endeavours to meet a dictionary definition of the word – "being entire or complete; entireness; a genuine or unimpaired state; honesty; uprightness in mutual dealings; probity". I am many things, but not a hypocrite.

Since 1974 it has been my weekend task to warden Steep Holm in its late twentieth century rôle as a nature reserve. Inherently and strategically it is an exceedingly important sanctuary and it is run as a tight ship along a course charted by the ideals and aspirations of the naturalist and broadcaster Kenneth Allsop.

A ferry to the island runs out of Knightstone Causeway, Weston-super-Mare, either an hour and a half before high-tide or a similar time after the water has turned, on most Saturdays and Bank Holiday Mondays from April to October. Booking details can be had from the Tourist Information Office at Beach Lawns on Weston seafront. The island, as will become clear in this book, is primarily cherished as wilderness, but there is also a place for humans.

"Holm" was the Viking word for an estuary island. If at times its name is rendered "Steepe Holmes" in Victorian fashion, or any other variation in spelling, I have left such inconsistencies because we tolerate idiosyncracies on this island.

Here I escape the word factory, from research as an historian and incarcerations at the typewriter, and sail back to permanent adolescence. Steep Holm has been a tithe on my life, its resources, and my writings. I hope that at times the spirit of the island will break through the verbiage and give you momentary flashes of the impetuous fury of romantic attachment.

R.L.
The Barracks, Steep Holm
County of Avon (detached)
1 iv 91

In the saddle:
Prime Minister
Henry John Temple,
third Viscount Palmerston,
commissioned the greatest
defences ever constructed
in the British Isles, but
died as the work began.
Painted, at the north
entrance to Westminster
Hall, by Henry Barraud
in 1865.

Palmerston Follies

When Viscount Palmerston [1784-1865] became Prime Minister for the second time, in June 1859, he appointed Sidney Herbert [1810-61] as his Secretary for War. It was the moment when the industrial revolution caught up with warfare. The French had begun the rapid construction of ironclad ships and with the outbreak of the Franco-Prussian war there were widespread rumours of imminent conflict between France and Britain. Sidney Herbert presented the British Cabinet with a contingency plan which assumed it would happen.

Weapons also were going through their metamorphosis from mediaeval to modern times. Rifled ordnance had to be introduced, for everything from carbines to cannon, and they would go through more changes in the 1860s than in all the centuries

7

since the first making of gunpowder. Outwardly, the appearance of the cannon would be transformed from the long, slender look of the past to a shape which is clumsy, fat and bulbous. The new guns appear pregnant.

The Royal Commission on the Defence of the United Kingdom reported in 1860 and recommended the building of what would become the chains of immense landward forts that protect the naval bases of Plymouth, Portsmouth and Chatham. Steep Holm was also to be fortified and garrisoned. The improved firepower of anti-ship guns, necessary to meet the threat from the ironclads, enabled a gun barrage to be established across the neck of the Bristol Channel to defend the ports of Cardiff, Newport and Bristol.

Geography made this possible between Weston-super-Mare and Penarth where Brean Down and Lavernock Point caused the narrowing of the waters. Effective blocking of the estuary was only possible, however, because of the existence, halfway across, of the strategically placed islands of Flat Holm and Steep Holm. The latter, of all four fortified points in the Bristol Channel, is by far the best preserved, with the distinction of being the only Victorian heavy battery in the British Isles that still has its guns.

The precise line that the Bristol Channel chain of forts would take, from Brean Down via Steep Holm and Flat Holm to Lavernock Point on the Welsh mainland, was announced by the War Department in January 1862. The begetters of these warworks would never see their creations. Sidney Herbert was soon sick and exhausted, and persuaded to go to the House of Lords, as Baron Herbert of Lea, but the peerage came too late to ease his burden. He was forced to resign from the War Department in July 1861, and was dead within a month.

Henry John Temple, third Viscount Palmerston, was voted £9,000,000 on 23 July 1860 for his package of fortifications. "If your dockyards are destroyed," he warned, "your navy is cut by the roots. If any naval action were to take place ... you would have no means of refitting your navy and sending it out to battle. If ever we lose the command of the sea, what becomes of this country?"

Palmerston's threat of sending his fleet to Italy kept Louis Napoleon from taking Genoa. At home he had to parry the opposition of his Chancellor of the Exchequer to the fortification programme. "Better," Palmerston wrote to Queen Victoria, "to lose Mr Gladstone, than to run the risk of losing Portsmouth." His statesmanship was the factor that kept Britain out of the

American Civil War by neutralising the heady enthusiasm of the English aristocracy for openly backing the Southern Confederacy. He was less successful in trying to keep Corfu for the British, in attempts to protect the territorial integrity of Poland – a lost cause even then – and in his efforts to mediate between Prussia, Austria and Denmark over the Duchies of Schleswig-Holstein.

Turbulent Europe contrasted with a quiet confidence at home. Palmerston died in October 1865 and three years later his massive fortifications were still being completed but there were no longer reasons for fearing an invasion of Britain. The national assortment of coastal defence works, which included fortifying the Irish port of Cork, were now collectively dubbed "Palmerston Follies". His other memorial is that there seems to be a Palmerston Road in every Victorian town in England.

An aside to the Steep Holm story is that another report had urged the development of Brean Down into the national station for turning round the West Indian mail packets. The first stone of Brean Down Harbour was laid by Lady Wilmot in 1864 but the impracticalities of the location were to be underlined by nature in the great storm of 9 December 1872 which carried away its stone pier. Undaunted, a new set of promoters put the Brean Down Harbour and Railway Act through Parliament in 1889, but as with Steep Holm the only Victorian transformation that would temporarily tame its remotest corner was to be the Palmerstonian war-works which would become reality in 1866-68.

Colonel Charles Kemeys Kemeys-Tynte, of Halswell, near Bridgwater, who had owned Steep Holm since the late 1830s, died in November 1860. It was Dame Anne Cooper, signing on behalf of his estate, who granted Her Majesty's Principal Secretary of State for the War Department the use of "parts or parcels" of Steep Holm "for the purpose of constructing batteries, fortifications, and other military works of public defence". Whitehall was thinking in the long-term and took a lease for 999 years, at the annual rent of thirty shillings for each acre the military used. There would be a royalty of sixpence for every ton of stone cut or quarried on the island and of a penny for every ton of imported stone that was "drawn over" the island.

John Perry, of Weston-super-Mare, was the builder who successfully tendered for the fortifying of Steep Holm and Flat Holm. It was on Steep Holm, with unseasonal urgency, that construction work commenced on 19 February 1866.

The navvies who began to build the Steep Holm fortifications in 1866 were visited by Thomas Steevens, a missionary for the Somerset Branch of the Navvy Mission. His memoirs, *The Fisherman and his Net* published in 1879, mention a number of visits. F.L. Loveridge, of the Somerset Archaeological and Natural History Society, has extracted the Steep Holm references.

14 May 1866: "Today I went to the Steep Holms. I first spoke to about ten men. I went to one of the huts in which the ganger lives: his name is Burgess ... I visited two other huts. The inmates received me kindly."

16 June 1866: "This morning [Saturday] I went to the Steep Holms. Arrived there about dinner-time ... Sunday morning I met most of the men in their lodgings in the huts ... On Monday, from the rough state of the weather, the boat could not leave Weston ... I collected the men together in the evening and held a service, when very few were absent. The number of men is increased, sixty or more are now employed on the Steep Holms ... The boat came on Tuesday."

30 June 1866: On Sunday morning I had an opportunity to visit the men at their homes. In one, ten were present, also the man and wife belonging to the hut with three children ... In another, the man and his wife with twelve lodgers were present ... In another, seven lodgers with the man, his wife, and two children ... I then went to the cottage which is connected with the Inn, where some of the men lodge. Present, eight men."

28 July 1866: "I went to Steep Holms. First visited Jonah Daws, the navvy who had been dangerously ill. He is now much better."

16 September 1866: "In the morning [Sunday] I went to the Flat Holms, from thence to the Steep Holms. Monday – I again visited most of the men and again tried to impress on their minds the necessity of attending to the things which we from time to time are permitted to hear."

13 October 1866: "I went first to the Steep Holms, remained there about an hour, visited some of the men and distributed a few tracts. I went from thence to the Flat Holms.... I returned again to the Steep Holms ... I returned to Weston in the evening."

16 October 1866: "I went from Brean Down to the Steep Holms. I visited most of the men at their work, I also gave tracts to a few. I also visited the people who occupy the huts. In one I read a portion of the Scriptures with some remarks, and left two tracts. In another I read Psalm 37, with remarks, and left a tract. In another read a tract and left others for the men to read. I also gave reading lessons to two of the children."

The frequent island hopping from Weston suffered inevitable disruption from the weather. There was also the loss of at least one of the supply vessels, Joan Rendell found as she went through Victorian newspapers: "The smack *Lucy Sarah* of Cardiff, laden with limestone for the works on Steep Holm, anchored off the island overnight and was blown across the channel and wrecked at Anchor Head, Weston-super-Mare, in 1866."

Among the inspectors of the work on Steep Holm in 1867 was Major-General William Wilberforce Harris Greathed [1826-78] of the Royal Engineers. He was a soldier of Empire with a record of heroism and luck. Born at Uddens Park, Dorset, he had as a young man been the first officer to force his way through the breach that ended the siege of Mooltan in the second Sikh war, on 2 January 1849. Whilst working as a consultant railway engineer at Allahabad he heard of the mutiny at Meerut and the rebel seizure of Delhi in May 1857. Orders came from John Russell Colvin, Lieutenant-Governor of the North-West Provinces, for Greathed to carry despatches and command a company of English volunteer cavalry. He became the first traveller from "Down Country" to ride the gauntlet into Meerut and later, taking messages from Colvin and Lord Canning, was the last European to find a way between Alygurh and Meerut for four months.

He led the left attack of the Delhi Field Force in the battle to take the ridge at Badlee-ka-Serai on 8 June 1857. The day nearly ended differently, when a small group of Britons found themselves surrounded by Pandees. Greathed drew his sword and led a rush that became a successful break-out as the enemy fled. He would be severely wounded, however, in the assault on Delhi. By the new year he recovered sufficiently to act as the Royal Engineer directing the crucial attack that broke the long siege of rebel-held Lucknow. British power restored, Greathed consolidated its grip by building more railways. He invaded China with Sir Robert Napier in 1860 and was in the vanguard of the campaign up to the capture of Pekin, at which point he returned to England with despatches.

Building great fortifications at Plymouth and moving on to put finishing touches to the work at Brean Down and on the islands in the Severn Estuary would round off his military career.

OVERLEAF, DOUBLE-PAGE SPREAD – **Twin barbettes of Palmerstonian Split Rock Battery, built 1866-68. Note the two cannon, which were abandoned by the military at the turn of the twentieth century and left lying in situ. Looking south across Bridgwater Bay to the Quantock Hills. Photographed by Colin Graham in 1975.**

Rudder Rock: entrance to Palmerstonian underground magazine, southern of two separated bunkers. Stencilled above the door is 'CARTRIDGE STORE FOR 7 IN. GUN.' Seen from the south-west. Photographed by Colin Graham in 1976.

Even on Steep Holm Victorian war-works were built on a monumental scale. Seawards, the outside of each barbette is embanked with spoil to just above parapet level, but on the island side the detail of the stonework is as perfect as you will find in any public building that graces a city concourse. For every barbette was faced on the inside by an arc of ashlars rounded to a 4 metre radius, 1 metre high and 5.4 metres across from end to end. The barbette walls are laid in snecked fashion, an urbane form of coursing with a jigsaw of tiny to huge blocks locking into a regular pattern.

This is sophisticated formal architecture, common in central London but rare, even in towns, in the West Country. All the blocks are faced to the same curve, squared at the edges into a flush border at the joins which contrasts with a protruding rough-cut centre. They were quarry-cut, I had assumed on the Mendip Hills, but my geological informants tell me the faced stone is from South Wales, which would certainly have been easier for shipment. They were then assembled on the island like a kit, with the island's own inferior rubble being used for backing, infill and uncoursed walling.

David Reece was a stonemason working on the island in 1868, perhaps with others, and he would have undoubtedly cut pieces of rock where necessary, but nowhere is there a working of the scale needed to have provided great ashlar blocks from Steep Holm itself in the quantity used in these gun batteries. Anyway, as the geologists have spotted, there are subtle differences between those and the island stone.

Four 12 cm eye bolts were set in the barbette walls at 50 cm from the concrete floor. These have 20 cm rings and were used, with ropes, to turn the gun carriage. This moved along a 7 cm thick circular rail track – known as a racer – which was set in the ground and has a diameter of 3.6 metres. At its centre, a C-pivot (the 'C' standing for cannon) a 15 cm obsolescent smooth-bore George III cannon, of 38 cm overall mouth diameter, was mounted vertically in the ground with just 60 cm of the barrel protruding above the concrete.

The only missing item in the equation, being the one part of the hardware of which there is not a single example surviving on Steep Holm, is the carriage on which the Victorian 7-inch, 7-ton rifled muzzle loaded cannon (RML Mark III, of Fraser pattern and Armstrong type) would have been mounted. These were Dwarf Traversing Platforms, described in the *Treatise on Military Carriages* of 1876. These are the details given for the type that were on Steep Holm, though as Major Richard Bartelot of the Royal Artillery Institution remarked: "It is difficult to say whether you will find anyone to understand them and I do not know of the existence of a platform that could be copied. I myself would have difficulty, not being an engineer." The accompanying detailed text is on pages 126 to 132 of the book, and the present chairman of the Kenneth Allsop Memorial Trust, John Percival, has since traced a collapsed carriage to its last resting place beside the entrance to the citadel in Cairo. These are the potted figures:

Type – 7 inch M.L.R. dwarf 'C', fitted with buffer.
Weight with gear – 80¼ cwts
Tonnage – 6.733 tons
Width between sides – 34½ in.
Nominal length – 15 ft.
Slope – 4 degrees
Diameter of trucks – 24 in.(Fore and hind)
Height from ground to axis of Trunnions – 5 ft. 8½ in.

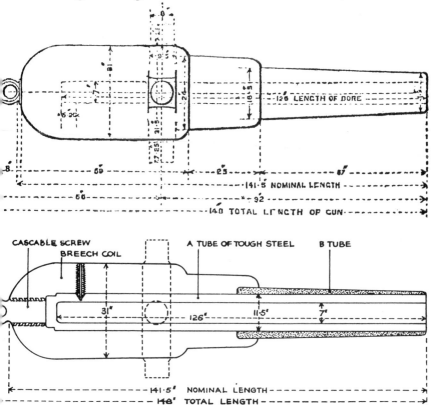

'The wrought iron muzzle-loading 7-inch gun of 7 tons, Mark III': composite version of contemporary drawings, with the measurements that prove the nine Palmerstonian gun barrels on Steep Holm are of this type. Redrawn by Arthur Killelay.

Left trunnion of a Palmerstonian gun barrel: with Woolwich serial number and proofing date – the markings stand for Royal Gun Factory, number 86, Mark III, 1868. This specimen is in the west barbette at Split Rock Battery (and is upside down). Seen from the east. Photographed by Colin Graham in 1975.

OPPOSITE – Gun No 86, Split Rock Battery West, and Elizabeth Fowles, the wife of author John Fowles: she died in 1990, and their Steep Holm story is in the 'Allsop Island' volume. Seen from the east. Photographed by Rodney Legg in 1973.

Gun No 67, Split Rock Battery East, and Edmund Mason: then chairman of the Steep Holm Trust which leased the island until the Kenneth Allsop Memorial Trust took over in 1974. Seen from the west. Photographed by Rodney Legg in 1973.

Lost and found: Victorian gun barrel No 79 and the platform built for the HMS Arrogant gun-armour tests in 1898. The cannon was 'lost' when the Battery Observation Post was built on top of it in 1941; and found with a metal detector in 1981. Seen from the east. Photographed by Leo Harrison Matthews in 1935.

Underground: Palmerstonian brick-clad magazine and stone stair-well beneath the east barbette at Split Rock Battery. Seen from the south. Photographed by Colin Graham in 1975.

Wonderful things are found with metal-detectors: Steve Tripp and the
Steep Holm work-force with newly-discovered Gun No 79, beneath the 1941-built
Battery Observation Post at Rudder Rock. Photographed by Colin Graham in 1981.

21

Displaced by the war: Victorian gun barrel No 97, from the east barbette of
Palmerstonian Summit Battery which was destroyed in the construction of Summit
Battery East (behind) in 1941. Seen from the north-east. Photographed by Colin
Graham in 1976.

Tombstone Battery: Palmerstonian gun barrel No 85, circular 'racer' and Georgian
cannon pivot for the carriage, but with the barbette having been largely stripped of its
stones in 1941. Seen from the north-west. Photographed by Colin Graham in 1976.

Cannon discovery: the Georgian pivot for the gun carriage in the Palmerstonian west barbette at Garden Battery, revealed by preliminary trenching. One heavy object that has to be moved is a 1941-built instrument pillar for gun-laying, to which a 1949 memorial plate is attached. Seen from the east. Photographed by Colin Graham in April 1976.

Presentable again: the west barbette of Palmerstonian Garden Battery, which had been completely filled with soil and rocks in the 1941 refortification of the island. Clearance revealed intact stonework and the 'racer' on which the wheels of the Victorian gun carriage were placed, as well as its cannon pivot. Seen from the east. Photographed by Colin Graham in June 1976.

Tombstone Battery: gun No 85, in the remains of its Palmerstonian single-barbette of 1866-68, with Salman Legg. Seen from the south. Photographed by Rodney Legg in 1991.

OPPOSITE – **Laboratory Battery: the western Palmerstonian barbette, with Victorian gun barrel No 72, after quantities of earth covering the rail and cannon-pivot had been cleared. Seen from the east. Photographed by Colin Graham in 1976.**

Laboratory Battery: the eastern Palmerstonian barbette, with Victorian gun barrel No 81, after clearance of Second World War debris and excess vegetation. Seen from the south-west. Photographed by Colin Graham in 1976.

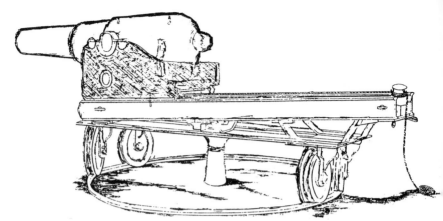

Palmerstonian C-pivot platform used for mounting the Steep Holm cannon: it turned on a circular rail and weighed as much as the gun itself. Redrawn from a Victorian print by Rodney Legg.

Underground, the magazine chambers in different parts of the island show considerable variations in layout, though all have vaulted brickwork. Ten survive intact (including the western one at Summit Battery, completely filled with 1941 rubble until it was dug out by a Forest School Camp in 1977). The pair at Rudder Rock have passages leading to an end chamber. Above the inner door of the southern magazine the woodwork still has its Victorian painted wording: "CARTRIDGE STORE FOR 7 in. GUN." The northern magazine has the word "Shell" instead of "Cartridge".

All six emplacements had to have double magazines, even for just a single gun barbette, because safety regulations required the cartridge charges (the propellant) to be stored separately from the shells (the explosive). Each storeroom is reached by its separate flight of steps at the rear of the emplacement and there are also vertical shafts that emerge to the side of the barbettes.

Only the twin magazines at Garden Battery were lost or destroyed during the 1941 re-fortification of the island though the barbettes suffered far more from the upheavals. Garden Battery East and Summit Battery East were completely devastated but all suffered some damage. At Split Rock Battery there was only minor stone robbing and that at Laboratory Battery, though on a much greater scale, has not overly spoilt the military archaeology.

Split Rock Battery is a gem and was scheduled by the Department of the Environment, as an ancient monument, in 1975. The position is particularly impressive, poised dramatically on the edge of a 200-foot craggy cliff, from the outcrops of which you can occasionally look down on a seal or a gannet, and with an open view of Exmoor and the Atlantic. Apart from the stone robbing at the approaches and the partial removal of a sidearms store it is complete still, with its shell and cartridge stores being perfectly preserved – though as the site was as ideal as the builders would find in the island they do not have the contorted passageways that were necessary to fit the constricted space at Rudder Rock.

The twin pair of magazines at Split Rock are fundamentally different, with the steps opening directly into the powder store. Here there are even unexpected differences between the rooms and one is longer than the other. In several of the chambers there are thick deposits of white snow-like efflorescent crystals leeched from the red brick. These layers do not dissolve in the stable, cool conditions, and similar accumulations have been found at the foot of walls in brick funeral vaults in London.

Considerable engineering works were necessary on the island before a start could be made hauling guns, equipment and supplies up the cliffs. Operations on Steep Holm must have encountered severe physical difficulties at every stage. There was a quay wall constructed above the rocky shore at the South Landing, though the present battered and apparently aged stone jetty was not added until 1942. The Victorians did, however, seem to have some heavy pier-type tressle construction seaward of their rubble wall, if only as part of a hoist platform. There is still at least one of its timbers embedded in the rocks. Even with that the quay could only have been operational within an hour of high water and then only at times when the sea was calm.

In front of the 1941-built searchlight post there is a curtain wall of rough island-blasted stone that was built in 1866. It runs for about 60 feet west of the searchlight post and is 5 feet high at the east. Behind it the ground has been embanked and plat-formed.

This was the island's dockside for the delivery of cut-stone and later for the arrival of the cannon. On the other side of the main quay wall, set back into the side of the cliff, is a limekiln. I have dismissed the suggestion of A.P. Ward and B.J. Murless in *Steep Holm, A Survey*, of 1981 that it might be earlier than 1866, because Steep Holm had no fuel supply with which to commer-cially produce lime. Nor, until the quayside hoist platform was built in 1866, any access for unloading fuel. Both features were first noted by the Ordnance Survey in 1883.

The limekiln was built by master-masons. Its arching and the

29

Palmerstonian Limekiln, at South Landing: beside a hoist platform which was used for landing fuel. Built in 1866. Seen from the south-east. Photographed by Colin Graham in 1977.

way the random rubble has been brought to courses is typical of the high standard of workmanship achieved on the island by the masons working for the War Department.

Their water for mixing the mortar would have come from the sea as this causes no structural problems except when concrete is put in direct contact with ironwork. But freshwater was obviously needed for drinking and other purposes and the underground Barracks reservoir would not be operational until after that building was erected and roofed.

The War Department surveyors found their freshwater trickling down a cavity in a haematite vein, about the high water mark, just over a hundred yards west from the South Landing limekiln.

The bottom of this cave – known now as Reservoir Cavity – was dammed in 1866 with stone to hold back the water. A winching point was built, again in stone, on the cliff edge above. It is a small square tower set into the slope. Two vertical grooves, built into the southern face, controlled ropes. It tapers towards the top which is 2.5 metres wide and 15 metres above the ledge from which the buckets were hauled.

Linking the top of the tower with the dockside platform there was a smoothly levelled trackway, about eight feet wide, which gradually descended, following the natural slant of the clifftop, to the limekiln. This track, which could have carried a railway line, is still well defined, despite rockfalls and minor landslips, and can be traced on the ground and from aerial photographs. As it arrives at the South Landing hoist platform area it passes directly to the north of the ruined wartime hut which stands behind the searchlight post.

A second limekiln was built at the top of the island, to the north of Parsons Cave and 120 feet south-west of the Tenement. This kiln, however, has not survived the 1941 re-fortification and is now just a crumbling inner bowl of bricks immediately behind the wartime generator house to the north-north-west of the 1941-built Garden Battery West.

Running north-west from the South Landing and on to the top of the island was a straight and steep incline that was constructed by the navvies to replace the existing but land-slipped mediaeval path to the west of the new cut. The monks' path zig-zags in five sections and is now covered with impenetrable scrub.

The incline is 350 feet from the top of the limekiln to the winching point beside the island's clifftop perimeter path. It had a winch installed in 1866 though that was removed early in the twentieth century and the present apparatus is its 1941 replacement.

Ditto the rails, which with their integral metal sleepers are, like the surviving rails on the east cliff, the metals of a German field railway that was brought to Steep Holm in 1941. Some temporary Victorian railway would have been laid up the incline, which is too steep to have walked up carrying heavy loads, but it would have had wooden sleepers in 1866. Its rails had been taken away by the time the Ordnance Survey team came to the island in 1883, for they show only a footpath.

Similarly around the rest of the island, there was no permanent Victorian railway system but prints and photographs of other construction work shows the navvies were adept at rigging up temporary tracks. I have even seen pictures of such transient railroads each side of what would become the permanent way, excavating it or building the embankment, where now there are only green fields beside the railway fences.

The other major project was the building of the Barracks. A shelf had to be blasted into the island's southern slopes, and there are numerous charge holes visible in the vertical cliff-face behind the building. Some blocks of rough stone with circular charge-holes are built into the north wall of the Barracks.

Between the building and that cliff is an underground reservoir, also built in 1867, holding 49,000 gallons. Rainwater runs down from the roofs, through a carbon filter bed, into a brick tank that is 16.7 metres long by 4.8 metres wide and 4.5 metres high with a vaulted roof.

It was a welcome explanation for the rather illogical position of the Barracks – it should have been built above the beach landing – that its position had been determined by the water supply. I quoted the theories of Colin Rogers, on the possibilities of hydrostatic pressure from the Mendip mainland, in *Steep Holm – a case history in the study of evolution* in 1978. Then in 1981 it rained, and kept on raining, and the tank got ever lower. I found that its inlets from the Barracks roof had been blocked – and thus ended an attractive theory!

There are granite keystones above the windows. Another keystone, above the western front-door, is carved in relief, "1867 V.R." – for the Queen, Victoria Regina. Similarly the dripstone sills to the windows are also in white granite. Unlike the limestone ashlars of the gun emplacements, the windows of the Barracks have gritty, greenish sandstone blocks at their sides, and similar Pennant-like stone was used for the corners of the building.

Palmerstonian Barracks: main door to the west section, with its dated keystone – 1867, Victoria Regina. Photographed by Colin Graham in 1974.

Palmerstonian Barracks: how it looked from 1946 to 1982, when major improvements took place. Looking west. Photographed by Colin Graham in 1974.

Palmerstonian Barracks: roofs and chimneys of the two 1867-built sections, seen from the north-west. Photographed by Colin Graham in 1974.

OPPOSITE – Palmerstonian Barracks: transformed into a baronial hall, with author John Fowles (second from right) holding court at the table. The collapsing ceiling had been removed to reveal the roof-trusses. Looking west. Photographed by Colin Graham in 1982.

OVERLEAF, DOUBLE-PAGE SPREAD – **Palmerstonian Barracks: main block, 1867-dated, with the addition of 1941-42 (near right, in brick) joining the two original sections. Seen from the south-east. Photographed by Colin Graham in 1981.**

Unexploded Victorian 7-inch shell: dumped in the mud beneath Tombstone Battery; marked 'PAL R' for 'Palliser Regular' and weighing 115 pounds. There are six side studs and a 3 cm screw plug at the base. John Pitfield's hand appears for scale. Photographed by Colin Graham in 1983.

OPPOSITE – Missing: the island's lost cannon. Its tenth Victorian gun barrel was next to the path at the top of the steps beside the original east barbette of the Palmerstonian Garden Battery. Note the cut-line, up the barrel, from the 1903 attempt by a Cardiff metal merchant to remove it in pieces. It was probably covered during the building of the present Garden Battery East in 1941. Seen from the south. Photographed by Leo Harrison Matthews in 1935.

Underground brick vaulting: Victorian reservoir, behind the Palmerstonian Barracks, built in 1866-67. Straw stalactites descend from the mortar. Beneath is a massive tank, 16.7 metres long and 4.8 metres wide, which contains 49,000 gallons of water. Seen from the east. Photographed by Colin Graham in 1978.

The random stonework at the Barracks is from the island but John Barrett is wrong, in *A History of Maritime Forts in the Bristol Channel*, when he says that the island "quarries would have provided all the necessary building stone required". The cut-stone is alien to the island. It is a darker grey and more gritty.

The buildings are, in John Barrett's imperial measure, 109 feet long by 20 feet wide. My reluctant first foray into metric produced a size of 37.5 metres long by 7.5 metres wide for the west wing, with walls 5 metres high in a single-storey, roofed to a central apex 6.5 metres above the ground. The east wing is of similar height, also with boarded roof and Welsh slates above, but is 12.5 metres long by 7.5 metres wide. There was a 7.5 metres extension to the east end, originally for latrines, which polluted the reservoir behind, and a 6.5 metres gap – roofed in 1941 – which separated the two wings.

The basic Victorian masonry is of 64 cm thick walls of random uncoursed island-dug stonework. Facings to the windows and doors are in Welsh ashlars. The building is brick-clad on the inside.

OPPOSITE – **Georgian cannon: re-mounted as a military showpiece beside the Palmerstonian Barracks, with cat beneath (Salman). Seen from the south. Photographed by John Pitfield in 1989.**

Georgian cannon: bang! Note the shell whizzing seawards (left edge) from John Pitfield's celebratory firing. Seen from the east. Photographed by Mary Cass in 1986.

Displaced 'racer': on which the wheels of the Palmerstonian gun carriage were set in the original east barbette of Summit Battery. Removed during the building of the present Summit Battery East in 1941, as was the cannon which is pictured opposite. Note the heavy claws which were set into the ground. Seen from the north. Photographed by John Pitfield in 1988.

OPPOSITE – Displaced George III cannon behind Summit Battery: it would be air-lifted to its present position outside the Barracks in 1986. Note the royal cipher midway between the breech and Daniel Percival's feet. Seen from the north. Photographed by Rodney Legg in 1973.

OVERLEAF, FIRST PAGE – Muzzle of the 24-pounder George III cannon: en route to its present location outside the Barracks. Seen from the south, immediately east of Summit Battery. Photographed by Colin Graham in 1982.

OVERLEAF, SECOND PAGE – Touch-down: a Sea King helicopter of 707 Naval Air Squadron. The pilot, Jerry Spence, lowers the Georgian cannon from Summit Battery on to a wooden carriage constructed by Ken Cass, as the guard-piece for the Palmerstonian Barracks. Seen from the east. Photographed by John Pitfield on 25 September 1986.

Gull and gun: the 24-pounder George III cannon from Summit Battery, re-mounted as a display-piece outside the Palmerstonian Barracks. Seen from the north-west. Photographed by Rodney Legg in 1989.

Mounted outside the Barracks is a 24-pounder Georgian cannon, made in about 1798 by Walker and Company of Rotherham. This particular barrel was turned into a showpiece long after both of Steep Holm's military phases had been consigned to history. It was brought to the island in 1866-68 as one of the C-pivots for the operational Victorian guns and it was never intended that much more than its mouth should be showing above the ground. That situation changed in July 1941 when 930 Port Construction Company of the Royal Engineers began to tear apart the east barbette of Summit Battery for the emplacement of a 6-inch naval gun.

The Georgian gun lay abandoned behind the concrete second-generation Summit Battery until 1980 when Chris Maslen began its tortuous rope-hauled progress into the cutting on the east side of the fortifications. As the gun was already displaced, rather than being in its archaeological context, the Allsop Trust had decided that it should be moved around the perimeter path to become the centrepiece outside the Barracks. Chris was wearing out the island's work force in the process and in 1986 Ken Cass intervened to take over the project. The rest of the journey was achieved in style, by a Sea King helicopter of 707 Naval Air Squadron, from Yeovilton, which in minutes had it bouncing to rest on the wooden carriage that Mr Cass had constructed. It was now pointing across Bridgwater Bay, at Hinkley Point nuclear power station.

John Pitfield stuffed a pound of gunpowder down the barrel. This sent a shell-shaped block of wood seawards at 400 mph. It splashed down about half a mile off the island. An iron projectile would have come from the gun at the same speed but with more inertia it would have travelled about six times the distance on a full charge.

The bore of the gun is 5.823 inches and its weight 5,544 pounds (2.475 tons), Victor Smith of the Fortress Study Group tells us. Its proper colour, he adds, is black, and the carriage would have been painted grey.

It is identical with those provided to HMS *Foudroyant*, launched in 1798, which was Nelson's flagship in the Mediterranean. She carried thirty-two 24 pounders on the main deck and thirty-two 23-pounders on the lower deck. Walker and Company also supplied the guns for HMS *Victory*.

Still lying at Summit Battery, from the same destroyed barbette as the air-lifted Georgian cannon, there is part of the 1869 gun's racer – the circular rail on which the gun platform ran – lying in an old railway cutting. It has massive three-feet wide claws set about three feet apart and this and the size of the Georgian cannon shows the amount of underground shock-resistance built into the Steep Holm emplacements.

Steep Holm was garrisoned by 7th Western Division of the Coast Brigade of the Royal Artillery. It had five gunners as the regular complement. One was a Master Gunner-in-charge. He no doubt delegated the daily task of airing the cartridge magazines – those with the gunpowder propellant charges – between the hours of nine o'clock in the morning and two o'clock in the afternoon, whenever the weather was dry, by opening the ventilation shafts.

The gunners wore the Royal Artillery uniform, which in those pre-khaki days was smart blue, for both jacket and trousers, with a red stripe down each flank. It would have brought the grey-green island a few splashes of real colour. Gentlemen and their servants still dressed for war.

Murderous weapons

Anti-ship guns had to keep pace with the evolution of the warship. France produced the first ironclad, *La Gloire*, and in 1859-60 the Royal Navy responded with HMS *Warrior*, which is now preserved in Portsmouth Harbour. She was an 80-gun ship with 400 feet of upper deck, twin funnels, three masts and 48,400 square feet of canvas. Warships and guns were both going through their sea-change.

The Victorian cannon that were brought to Steep Holm in 1868-69 were totally a product of that decade. Their pedigree is American and they were battle-proven. The stimulus for the development had been the Civil War and in use with the Union army those predecessors of the Steep Holm guns would prove murderous.

Guns of this type were invented by a West Point graduate, Robert Parker Parrott [1804-77], who left the American army to run a foundry. In 1861 he perfected a method of strengthening the existing cast-iron guns by shrinking wrought-iron hoops on the breech. They could now take a far greater charge and at the same time Parrott introduced an expanding projectile for rifled cannon. Production went ahead immediately, and Parrott guns were used by the Union army against Confederate forces throughout the Civil War, which lasted until 1865.

Details of Parrott's two gun patents were soon being studied on this side of the Atlantic by engineers Sir William Armstrong (inventor of the breech loader) and Sir Joseph Whitworth (who standardised screw threads). Whitworth experimented with hexagonal rifling in muzzle-loaded guns. An elongated projectile was then used to increase the range and precision of fire. Traditional cannon balls had become a thing of the past. They were replaced by cartridges devised by Major William Palliser [1830-82].

Lynall Thomas suggested in Britain that Parrott's wrapping of a strengthened tube around the exteriors of the guns could be improved upon. The wrought-iron element should be at the centre to receive the initial impact. Palliser, improving his reputation as a scientific artillerist (he was later knighted), placed the wrought-iron tube in the middle of the gun and found this "added enormously to the strength". Thomas made the world's first 7-inch gun – of steel and forged in one piece, "the largest which had ever been attempted" – but the breech burst with its second trial charge.

In 1865 the Royal Gun Factory at Woolwich made its first

heavy rifled muzzle-loaders and they evolved into the massive seven-ton barrels that lie on Steep Holm. These guns, the Rifled Muzzle Loaded Mark III, were designed for land service and were standard issue for most forts, with a production run of about 500. Fifty-one had been made of the Mark I, but only two prototypes of the Mark II, and the Mark III differed in being constructed by the Fraser method, devised by R.S. Fraser, which was a simplified version of Sir William Armstrong's design. Both the Mark I and Mark III have wrought iron casings and an inner tube of tough steel, but the Mark II used a tube of coiled iron instead.

Mark III – the gun that went into service – has a calibre of seven inches, an overall length of 12 feet 4 inches and a bore of 10 feet 6 inches. Inside the rifling consists of "Three grooves, 1.5 inch wide and .18 inch deep, with a uniform twist of one turn in 35 calibres". The groove was rounded off at both sides, a Woolwich refinement, as this prevented the steel splitting along the edges. Two studs, projecting from the muzzle of several of the Steep Holm guns, were locating pegs for a cradle or tray. The shell was placed on to this and aligned with the rifling of the gun.

These were the last generation of muzzle-loaded guns. They were never used in anger but that sort of retrospective comment is relative. One hopes to be alive to write the same, one day, as the epitaph to the nuclear bomb.

"How did they ever get those guns up here?" is a question I am repeatedly asked. Unfortunately we don't know. John Barrett suggests that they were probably unloaded one at a time from a lighter, immediately beneath each barbette, using sheers positioned up the cliff. Nail-biting but practical – and at least it was the direct route, rather than using the narrow and tortuous island paths. The gunners of the Coast Brigade had the experience and the nerve to do it, though in 1870 a detachment on Malta ran out of luck and had one death and several injured when a hoist cable snapped and a 12-ton gun barrel slid down the cliff.

Identification of the Steep Holm guns with the "Wrought Iron Rifled Muzzle Loading 7 inch Gun of 7 tons, Mark III" as depicted in plate V IA of the "R.M.L Guns in the Service" section of the *Treatise and Construction of Ordnance*, 1877, was confirmed in 1975 by Major Richard Bartelot of the Royal Artillery Institution at Woolwich. He had earlier said these were not the ones lying on Steep Holm, as a result of misinformation from "two or three people who have been interested in the ordnance deposited there" but he had to revise his opinion when I provided the overall length of the gun – 148 inches. This ruled out the 133 inch "7 inch Gun of 6½ tons, Mark III".

As for the Steep Holm version and its immediate prototypes, the *Treatise* has this to say about the "7-inch R.M.L. Gun of 7 tons" on pages 192 to 194:

"There are three patterns of this gun. This nature is entirely a land service gun, and was introduced in 1865 as a battering gun for coast defence.

"Mark I is built on the original construction, and externally is similar to the 7-inch 6½ ton gun, Mark I. The 'B' tube of this pattern is covered by an additional thin coil so as to reduce the preponderance, which was found to be excessive. 51 were manufactured.

"Mark II. Introduced in 1866, consists of same parts as Mark II, 7-inch 6½-ton gun. Previous to April 1868 these guns were marked F.II. on the left trunnion.

"Mark III, introduced in 1866, differs only in length from Mark III, 7-inch 6½-ton gun. Previous to April 1868 these guns were marked F.II. on the left trunnion."

'A' tube was the toughened steel bore.'B' tube was the outer casing of the muzzle. The other matter cleared up by Major Bartelot was the mistaken attribution of the design of the Steep Holm guns to Sir Joseph Whitworth: "He is not often credited with producing cannon used by the services – preference was given to William Armstrong."

So, it had finally been established, Steep Holm possessed eight of the ten 7-inch 7-ton Mark III Armstrong-designed rifled muzzle loaded gun barrels that had been emplaced on the island. A search was mounted to find the other two.

In 1978, in *Steep Holm – a case history in the study of evolution*, I predicted that one of the island's missing Victorian gun barrels survived beneath the later war-works at Rudder Rock or in the sea below the cliffs:

"Enough later activity, including the building of a searchlight post on the side of Rudder Rock, has taken place to hide the gun. A metal detector might find it, and while the sub-surface litter of ironwork is considerable, a lump weighing seven tons should register a stronger signal. A sea magnet may also be necessary as the precipitous cliff on the north side of Rudder Rock is the only place in the entire island where anything pushed over the edge will fall into deep water. This could have been the most tempting method of disposal."

The sea-search at one of the so-called lowest tides of the

century drew a blank, and instead we dug beneath the 1941-built Battery Observation Post. Ken Thorne led the way and disappeared into a tunnel beneath its concrete floor. Loose stones trickled down on him and caution had to bring the operation to a halt.

It was in 1981 that we were at the point of giving up. Stan Rendell had been misled by a wartime informant, who had the somewhat inexplicable notion that a seven ton weight beneath the floor would make it unstable, into writing in *Steep Holm, A Survey*, that "it is unlikely that the old cannon would have been buried in the concrete of the emplacements as is sometimes suggested".

I borrowed Steve Tripp's metal detector and went inside the Battery Observation Post. There was a signal immediately but it proved to be a pipe, which was fortunate as I feared the building might have steel-bar reinforcements set into the concrete of the floor. It did not, and thirty seconds later there was no signal until a third of the way into the building where the machine screeched and the pointer swung to the right and went off the scale. I kicked old gull nests to mark the breech-shape of a gun. I could get no signal from the actual barrel which though only a few inches lower is much narrower. Then I ran back to the Barracks and in the three hours that were left before our return boat Richard and Steve Tripp chipped away slowly at the concrete to reveal what at the end of the afternoon was just one square inch of rust. This was no discarded piece of corrugated iron – a tap from the bar had the resonance of striking the island itself, and there was the unique curve of the fat end of a gun barrel.

Number 79, of 1869, it turned out to be in the weeks that followed; it is intact apart from a trunnion which was blown off in the gun-test which took place in 1898.

The other missing Victorian gun barrel, along with its George III cannon-pivot, is at Garden Battery East. Or, underneath it – now we know that the Royal Engineers did not mess with moving the odd seven tons when they could simply cover it. Even without it, the island's total of nine of these huge guns is impressive enough, particularly as most of those on neighbouring Flat Holm have been cut-up or removed. On the mainland the situation is worse and cannon of this type are now virtually extinct. The last "preserved" specimens were taken for scrap in 1940.

Overseas there are isolated colonial survivors; reputedly on Malta, outside a fort in Cairo, and one or two on Ascension

Island in the mid-Atlantic. Even if those are taken into account it is only on Steep Holm that there is a virtually intact collection and they are in an almost perfect condition.

Their rarity was confirmed by a Department of the Environment official in 1974 whose report stressed "the very great importance placed upon the muzzle-loading gun barrels that survive on the island." Preservation is urged: "These [cannon] are indeed rare and should be cherished as if they were ancient monuments." Historically, the significance of the guns of Steep Holm is that they were among the largest and last muzzle-loaders ever made. Size with these guns is a relative matter, and cannon of the same basic shape were built to 80 tons and exist on Malta and Gibraltar. Nothing of this enormous weight was thought to have survived in Britain, but in 1976 port construction workers at Dover uncovered an 80-ton gun in its original emplacement. Unlike the Steep Holm cannon, which were revolved manually, the Dover gun was pulled around its mounting by a steam engine.

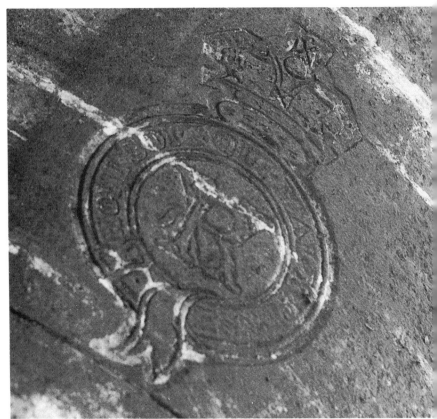

'Shame on him who thinks evil of it': a loose translation of the motto of the Order of the Garter from Queen Victoria's cipher, on gun No 97 of 1869. Photographed by Rodney Legg in 1973.

Each Steep Holm barrel has 38 lines incised for aiming purposes, and three holes for sighting pins, while the left trunnion carries the proofing year and Woolwich serial number. At the centre of each gun, on the top, is Queen Victoria's cipher and the wording "HONI SOIT QUI MAL Y PENSE" – the motto of the Order of the Garter, in mediaeval French meaning "shame on him who thinks evil of it". The letters are surmounted by St Edward's crown. The details stamped on the guns are usually visible in cases where the appropriate part of the gun is exposed, particularly if rubbed with moist leaves, but most now lie upside down. The royal cipher is best seen on the breech of the gun at Summit Battery East.

Remarkably, despite being in the salt air for a century, the guns are well preserved and brown only from a light surface rusting. The toughened casing successfully resists corrosion, unlike the younger but rapidly flaking ironwork from the Second World War, which is in an advanced stage of disintegration all over the island. Even the heavy armour-plated doors of the generator houses have rusted away.

These are the trunnion stampings of the Steep Holm batch, with "R-G-F" being the Royal Gun Factory, at Woolwich, and "III" signifying Mark III barrels. The numbering would have been done when the gun was proofed, after its test firings:

Split Rock Battery East: "R-G-F   No 67   III   1869"
Split Rock Battery West: "R-G-F   No 86   III   1868"
Rudder Rock: "R-G-F   No 79   III   1869"
Summit Battery West: "R-G-F   No 87   III   1868"
Summit Battery East: "R-G-F   No 97   III   1869"
Laboratory Battery West: "R-G-F   No 72   III   1869"
Laboratory Battery East: "R-G-F   No 81   III   1869"
Tombstone Battery: "R-G-F   No 85   III   1869"
Garden Battery East: (gun barrel lost)
Garden Battery West: (details illegible)

Such guns would normally have been provided with sufficient ammunition for a day's firing – estimated at two hundred rounds per gun – but John Barrett has suggested that this figure was probably increased for islands, to allow for the probable impossibility of re-supply. On the other hand there does not seem to have been much storage space. The shell magazines could not have been racked much more than a metre from the floor in view of the weight of the projectiles. This was a cylindrical shot, of typical shell-shape, that weighed 115 pounds (52 kilos). They were known as Palliser shot, after Major (later Sir) William Palliser, and were fired with a 30 pound charge of gunpowder. These shells, which are 40 cm long, have a solid head that punched into its target. There is no fuse – they relied upon frictional impact for detonation. They could go through eight inches of plate, the armour of an ironclad warship, at a range of a thousand yards.

These shells carry the markings "PAL R" – Palliser Regular – and have six side studs and a 3 cm screw plug at the base. Some still lie off the island. Comments Major David Benger: "They could hardly have been fired there. My guess is that they were dumped, perhaps when the RML guns were dismantled."

It is not just in retrospect that Steep Holm and the other great war-works had become Palmerston Follies. The epithet was already in use in 1869. Britain's fear of wars was already receding into far-flung pink patches of the globe as the Empire brought ever-expanding horizons. The War Department put Steep Holm into its care-and-maintenance category, greased and gunned but only operated by a token garrison, from its completion onwards. Census returns record a population of six in 1871, five in 1881, nine in 1891 and five in 1901. France was no longer the instant enemy and by 1879 the popular clamour was for war with Russia, after both Britain and Russia had intervened in Afghanistan:

> "We don't want to fight, but, by jingo if we do,
> We've got the ships, we've got the men,
> And we've got the money too!"

If the Russians had suddenly sailed up the Bristol Channel there was no way the island gunners could have repulsed them other than by firing from one barbette and then running on to the next.

Had there been warning of an emergency, Steep Holm would have received reinforcements from units of part-time gunners. These, on the English side of the Bristol Channel, were the 1st Gloucester and Somerset Artillery Volunteers, the 2nd Gloucester Engineer Reserves, and the Royal Navy Artillery Volunteers. All were organised from Bristol.

Channel swimmer

A moment of madness resulted in one of triumph on a cold day in September 1875. Henry Garrett, at the age of twenty-six, had become the first person to successfully complete the swim from Weston-super-Mare to Steep Holm. He found, however, that it was impossible to swim through the choppy tide race to land on the island beach – the reason that the Allsop Trust discourages swimming – and had to embark on an almost complete circuit of the island, around the northern cliffs and Rudder Rock, to the calmer water off the South Landing.

There the island's master gunner was waiting on the rocks. Allowing for tidal drift, Garrett had managed eight miles – in a time of 2 hours 16 minutes. The gunner provided a quasi-military salute by firing his shotgun. That at least alerted the Inn to heat the coffee.

Garrett was rubbed down and wrapped in blankets and then bundled into a rowing boat for the last part of his voyage to the Inn. After several drinks, and sandwiches, he had enough energy to climb on to the top of the island to look down on the scene of his victory. The rowing boat took him back to Weston.

Top brass inspection

Steep Holm was inspected on 9 June 1881 by a joint-services committee headed by Vice-Admiral Augustus Phillimore and Vice-Admiral Boys for the Royal Navy, and Sir Digby Murray, Colonel J.H. Smith and Major Crozier for the Royal Artillery and the Royal Engineers. Their vessel, a steamer, was loaned for the occasion by the third Marquis of Bute, the re-builder of Cardiff Castle.

Field Club visits

The countryside was being re-discovered by the Victorians through their field club excursions which explored the world that was celebrated in both its pastoral timelessness and brutal rawness in naturalistic canvases for their living rooms. T.H. Thomas visited the island with a party from Cardiff Naturalists' Society on 29 May 1883, timed to catch the last of Wild Peony bloom, and sketched a scene that the official transactions would also record in Romantic Movement phraseology reminiscent of several years before: "A black-eyed maiden, embrowned by the

Peonies, leeks, and a monk's memorial stone: drawn by T.H. Thomas during an expedition of Cardiff naturalists to Steep Holm on 29 May 1883 – 'A black-eyed maiden, embrowned by the sun and breezes that breathe and blow around her island home, is charged by the landlady to guide us to the spot where the sacred plant grows.'

sun and breezes that breathe and blow around her island home, is charged by the landlady to guide us up to the spot where the sacred plant grows."

They came in style. For she, and the Wild Peonies on the cliff-edge, are depicted with a paddle-steamer anchored below.

Military Steep Holm co-existed with the Victorian leisure industry. That can be taken to infer carefree pre-terrorist days but in fact Queen Victoria was the British monarch who survived the most assassination attempts – seven at the final count.

Steep Holm and Flat Holm were still capable of being brought back into active service. This was tested later in 1883 when a garrison battery of the Royal Artillery sailed across to the islands from Newport. They stayed two days.

"Some excellent practice was made," reported the Weston Mercury of 29 September 1883. "The booming of the guns could be distinctly heard eastwards for fully 15 miles, whilst within that distance the vibrations caused by the explosions were distinctly felt."

The Davies year

In the summer of 1885 Caroline Davies and her sons Harold and Wallis came to Steep Holm, and in a year of what must have been titanic effort, made the island more than just agriculturally self-sufficient. They grew garden produce and vegetables of all kinds, as well as oats and barley, and mowed the uncropped parts of the top of the island for hay to keep their livestock. The animals included three heifers, one steer, five goats, ten pigs, poultry and a donkey,

They had a pilot cutter, the *Lance*, which was kept moored off the island, as well as four flat-bottomed fishing boats which were raised up a rock slipway, upon which the beach wall was constructed in 1941. *Spray*, a Weston yacht, came across weekly with stores for the island's eight-man military garrison and the inn. The island had a regular winter fishing industry, employing up to eight men. Nets strung across the shingle caught principally sprats and whiting. Hook lines were set for conger, skate and cod. Catches sometimes reached three tons per tide, and fish were taken to Cardiff market by the island's cutter.

Then it was over. Mrs Davies's boats, furniture and animals were bought for £250 in July 1886 by Thomas Hall, formerly landlord of the Crown Inn at Glastonbury. He took over the island's tenancy from Mrs Davies, at a rent of £35 a year, and things again lapsed into obscurity.

'Observatory Battery'

A mystery in the records is the island's phantom Observatory Battery. This was never built. It is shown, however, on the large rolled masterplan of the island housed in the Public Record Office, and located halfway along the north face of the island, almost equal in distance between Summit and Laboratory batteries. On this map, however, a question mark is added after the name, and a comment at the foot of the map – "subject to survey" – applies to both Observatory and Summit batteries. On the ground at the former, there are not only no guns, but no sign of any emplacements, or of later work to displace them. The proposal was included by the Inspector General of Fortifications in his review of the Western District Coast Defence Armaments, presented on 1 December 1888, though it was not given a name.

The presumption must be that Observatory Battery was never started, and militarily it would have been the least necessary of all, as it is well covered by the arcs of fire from both Summit and Laboratory guns. Anyway, the distance along the southern shore between Split Rock and Garden batteries is appreciably longer than that separating Summit from Laboratory. The Barracks is at the middle of the southern side but cannot be counted as a fighting or even defensive structure. The negative evidence for no Observatory battery is that the five known sets of emplacements can account for all ten of the island's guns.

Explanations of Steep Holm's original military layout have to be supported by reference to the Victorian plans. Twentieth century maps and accounts have introduced inaccuracy and confusion. It this account, as you go clockwise around the island, the batteries have been named Rudder Rock, Summit, Observatory (no trace), Laboratory, Tombstone, Garden and Split Rock.

Among the lesser military relics on Steep Holm are carved stone boundary posts. These are of Palmerstonian rather than Second War vintage and were intended to show the extent of military occupation. Some are incised with "W.D." for the War Department, and the government's broad arrow. Politics meant the Royal Artillery had to be seen to be occupying only the minimum area of land essential for its needs. Each gun battery plot was therefore carefully squared up and marked out. On Steep Holm the exercise was meaningless, as the whole island had to be used in various ways, but it was a regulation that was carried out all the same. In 1941, when the military returned, they would have the island to themselves.

Marconi's first signal over water

The world's first radio transmission across water was beamed beside Steep Holm in 1896. It was sent by Guglielmo Marconi [1874-1937] from Brean Down on the English mainland to Lavernock Point, Penarth; a distance of nine miles. He already realised the potential of his discovery and by November 1896 had established the Wireless Telegraph Company Limited at the Needles, Isle of Wight, as the world's first permanent wireless installation.

The 'Arrogant' attack

In 1898 the War Office chose Steep Holm for a test that was to establish its own obsolescence. Breech-loading guns were now replacing cannon and in 1898 the Admiralty decided to see whether the new guns could be put into existing barbettes with metal shields for additional protection. This had the advantage of being considerably cheaper than making new emplacements. Rudder Rock, at the west point of the island, was chosen for the exercise. A dummy 9.2-inch breech-loader was placed in a specially-made 'tortoise' shield of nickel steel thirty-four feet from end to end. This metal was three inches thick, of the type used for armoured plate in battleships from a process invented in America by Hayward Augustus Harvey [1824-93]. It had seven per cent nickel to give it extra strength. The tortoise-shape was chosen so that the surface curving inwards would offer least resistance and deflect shot. The front was oval and the whole shield moved on wheels, running on the racer of the 1868 emplacement.

The shield and barbette at Rudder Rock were pounded by HMS *Arrogant*, a second-class cruiser, using her whole armament of 6-inch, 4.7-inch and smaller guns. The *Arrogant* was a twin screw ship laid down on 26 May 1896 and built at Devonport. This date shows that John Barrett was in error, in *A History of the Maritime Forts in the Bristol Channel*, in stating that the "partial destruction by HMS *Arrogant* of Rudder Rock" was "in 1881". She was 320 feet long with 5,000 tons displacement, and was to survive the First World War, being broken up at Blyth in 1923.

What happened is reported in the *Naval and Military Records* for 25 August 1898: "After many days the *Arrogant*, steaming at about ten knots in the teeth of wind at a distance of 1,800 yards from Steep Holm fired four of her starboard guns in quick succession, clouds of dust being seen to rise from the rock in the vicinity of the battery, though, so far as binoculars could reveal, no flash hits were made. Indeed experts declared that it would need almost magnificent gunnery to drop a shot on to the battery, so great is its elevation above sea level.

"As the *Arrogant* swept past her big 6-in gun was brought into range, the weapon going off with a deafening roar, then the *Arrogant* steamed slowly round the island. As it reached its south-western extremity a heavy report was heard from [observers at] the Summit Battery, which was generally regarded as a signal that no hit upon the shield had been made.

"Again the cruiser shaped her course past the battery and again she fired and thus the firing continued from eight o'clock until noon. The earlier stages of the experimental firing, namely for about the first two hours, appeared to have been carried out with guns of a smaller calibre, for so far no effect was produced upon the target or breast-work of the fort.

"Towards noon however, some of the heavier defence ordnance were brought into use and these quickly made their effect felt, for so far as spectators at a distance could observe a portion of the shield was blown away causing the gun to be exposed and the surrounding structure to be reduced to a mere heap of rubbish. It is estimated that nearly 200 shells were fired from the cruiser. Shortly after mid-day the firing ceased and the *Arrogant*

Channel firings: remains at Rudder Rock of the experimental Harveyed-steel 'tortoise shell' gun-shield of 1898, blown to pieces by HMS Arrogant. To the right is a George III cannon muzzle and the 1941-built Battery Observation Post. Seen from the south. Photographed by Colin Graham in 1975.

returned to her anchorage." The report is unclear in its reference to "heavier defence ordnance" – land guns – which it suggests the cruiser was carrying. Her own armament had nothing heavier than the 6-inch gun which she was already using.

The shield and dummy gunners were blown apart, leaving the mock 9.2-inch gun exposed and demolishing 1.2 metres of concrete. Most of the smashed armour was removed and taken for examination to the Old Ranges at Shoeburyness, Essex. Three large plates of 89 mm backing metal remain in the barbette at Rudder Rock. One is rent with a fracture more than 60 cm in length, the second has a number of strick-stabs, and the third is undamaged. I am told that little Harveyed steel of this quality survives and that these chunks at Rudder Rock may well be unique.

Because of the "historical significance of the site" the Department of the Environment announced in 1975 it was scheduling the Rudder Rock battery as an ancient monument and added: "The remains of the shattered 'tortoise-shell' are very much part of the monument in their existing positions." This scheduling allowed Steep Holm to claim the contradictory superlative "the youngest ancient monument in Britain", though only temporarily as the Deparment then listed a Second World War tank-trap in Dorset.

Out with a bang

Technology was catching up with the Severn's barrage of guns by the 1890s. Cordite, the supercharged shell propellant, had been invented in 1888. The motor torpedo boat was now in the naval arsenal and could sweep in at 20 knots. As John Barrett says, in *A History of Maritime Forts in the Bristol Channel*, "it would have been extremely difficult for the RML guns to depress low enough to fire on them if they were passing close to the island". Or quickly enough, he might have added. He points out that the gunners would have been disabled by dusk and continues: "It was, therefore, proposed that in time of war two harbour defence ships with four gunboats and four torpedo boats would be permanently stationed in the Channel. Had Steep Holm been retained by the military it would have needed breech-loaded guns".

The chain of Bristol Channel forts were destined to be stood down in 1901 but they would literally go out with a bang. Gunner Haines, whose home was in Bridgwater, had been posted from Steep Holm to Brean Down at the end of June 1900. He was not at all happy there and a week later took a carbine from above the bed of Gunner Kehoe. Haines then went to number three magazine and fired the gun down the ventilator shaft into "pretty well three tons of powder". He was fatally injured in the bang which was heard by his former mates on Steep Holm. Verdict: "Temporary insanity."

The obsolete muzzle-loaders on Steep Holm were sold by the War Office, in 1903, to a Cardiff scrap merchant. He found them too heavy to move and attempted cutting but failed to break them into pieces. Both guns at Garden Battery were attacked with determination and became increasingly resistant as the cutter approached the centre and "the intensely hard inner lining of the bore". Something may have been taken back to Cardiff, however, as all the mountings for the guns have completely disappeared.

Steep Holm was not the only fortification where the guns were abandoned. The six 9-inch rifled muzzle-loading guns of the Palmerstonian Needles Battery, at the western tip of the Isle of Wight, were pushed over the cliffs. In 1978, after it had acquired the Needles headland, the National Trust announced that it planned to raise the two barrels which remained in the sea on the southern side of the fort. They were still in the water when the Prince of Wales declared the battery reopened on 9 June 1982 but I take it that it will be only a matter of time before Steep Holm loses its unique claim to be the only Victorian battery with its heavy guns. Their guns are heavier than ours, at 12-tons, and fired a 256 lb. shell with a charge of 50 lbs. of gunpowder.

Francis Blathwayt's birds

Around the turn of the twentieth century, Reverend Francis Linley Blathwayt became the first ornithologist to visit Steep Holm frequently. He was compiling the bird notes for Somerset's *Victoria County History*, but the bulk of his records are unpublished in voluminous diaries. He sailed out from the River Axe, passing the Uphill ferry and Brean Down, and had more luck with crossing to the island on or around my birthday than I ever manage. Perhaps there has been a climatic change! Blathwayt was to have a long life, equally full of bird noting, and would return to Steep Holm with a party from Bristol Naturalists' Society on 2 May 1936.

These are his jottings from the turn of the century, which I have transcribed in full from the original diaries, by courtesy of Colonel Evelyn Prendergast:

18 April 1898: "List of birds noticed on Steepholm. Peregrine Falcon (nesting on the north side), Kestrel, Wheatear, Coal Tit, Meadow Pipit (common), Rock Pipit, Swallow (several), Sand Martin, Willow Wren, Starling (small flock), Skylark (common), Greenfinch, Herring Gull (several nests, one egg, on north-west side), Lesser Black-backed Gull (a few pairs, on north-west side)."

18 April 1899: "2 Scaup Ducks – off Brean Down. Ravens apparently nesting again, west of old nest."

20 April 1899: "Peregrine Falcon – Steep Holmes – pair, nest and 4 eggs. (The eggs were laid on a ledge about the middle of the north face. Cliff sheer for about 90 feet, and the eggs were laid about 20 or 30 feet above high water. The hen bird flew round chattering, but the male kept some distance away. The eggs were hard set. According to one of the soldiers on the island, another pair of Peregrines were nesting on the west face of the island but we did not see them.) Lesser Black-backed Gull, Herring Gull (about 16 pairs nesting, and rather more *Larus argentatus* than *L. fuscus*. We found plenty of nests, some quite finished, but 20 eggs had been laid. There were several gulls in immature plumage about the island. Nests on the west end of north face.) Starling – a small flock (we found one dead, evidently killed by the Peregrine). Skylark – several. Rock Pipit – several. Sheldrake – many around the island, and some were evidently thinking of nesting somewhere on the north side. Sand Martin – several. Swallow – a few."

20 April 1900: "Redstart – several males. Wheatear – several males. Greater Whitethroat. Chiffchaff. House Sparrow – a few. Blackbird, Rock Pipit – several. Meadow Pipit. Skylark – several. Starling – flock of about 17. Linnet (or Greenfinch) – a few flying about. Kestrel – a pair (south side). Peregrine Falcon – a pair (north side. We let H. down to the ledge where these birds nested last year. He saw freshly killed birds near, and a new hollow had been scraped in the ledge but no eggs had been laid. On this day last year there were 4 considerably incubated eggs, so the birds had this year either laid in a different place or were much later in laying. The birds did not fly round us chattering, but kept far away until we had moved on, when one of them returned.) Herring Gull – about 10 or 12 pairs, just beginning to build (counted 18 together). Lesser Black-backed Gull – I only saw 1 or 2 pairs, but as the gulls seemed later in building this year, they were perhaps away fishing. Cormorant – a pair, west end of island. One flew out from the side of the cliff, and circled

round, just above the waves, as if anxious to return. Was perhaps nesting. Sheldrake – a few flying about near the island, also a few small gulls (Kittiwakes or Black-headed young).

25 June 1901: "Herring Gull, Lesser Black-backed Gull – about 23 pairs breeding on the cliffs at the north-west end. Rather more Herring Gulls than Lesser Black-backed Gulls. Also a few in immature plumage. F.G.S. got an egg. Cormorant – saw 5 together. They were, I think, one adult and 4 young. They probably breed on the island, and from the fishy smell at the north-west end of the island, that is their favourite haunt. Peregrine Falcon – a pair breeding in usual place, viz in the middle of the north face. From their behaviour probably had young. Larks, Meadow and Rock Pipits, a few Sheldrakes also seen on the island."

13 July 1904: "Went round Steep Holmes by steamer from Weston. A good many gulls, both Herring Gulls and Lesser Black-backed were nesting on the north face. Young appeared full feathered. Think I caught a glimpse of one of the Peregrine Falcons."

18 April 1907: "Went to Steep Holm in *Sylori*. Had to row all the way there, and sailed back with very least breeze. Sea smooth. Hot sun all day, no wind. Peregrine Falcon – pair nesting on cliffs on the north side of island, below the Chapel Rock. Male bird swept away. Falcon sat close. We rowed along under the cliff shouting and clapping our hands but she did not leave the nest until we were exactly below her, when she flew from a hole in the cliff not very far above high water, and circled round chattering loudly. I did not see the male bird return, but he was on the island when first we arrived. Bird probably had laid set eggs. Raven – a pair were with nest and well grown young apparently nearly ready to fly, on steep cliff to the north of old Inn. Nest built not far above the water at the north-east corner of the island. Impossible to reach without a rope. Two old birds flew croaking above the nest. Kestrel – one seen on the south side of the island. Mobbed by the Raven and driven away over the sea. Herring Gull – numbers have I think increased of late. I saw quite 25 pairs of adults about the island and should think that there were probably nearly 30 pairs of nesting birds. Chief nesting haunt was on the east end of the north cliff. Some were building at the west end above the Rudder Rock, and had started scraping nests. Saw one or two immature birds about. Lesser Black-backed gull – I only noticed 2 or 3 pairs. Perhaps more arrive later in season. Cormorant – I think I noticed two of these birds flying over the sea near the island, just as we were landing. Sheldrake – only about 6 pairs about the island. They

do not breed here in large numbers, as on Brean Down. Other birds noticed on the island were – Wren(2); Robin; Blackbird (female); Starling (12); Skylark (a few); Rock Pipet (several); a pigeon flew over, I think it was a Stock Dove. We rowed all round the island under the cliffs."

Additionally, on 18 April 1907, Blathwayt made a brief mention of the island's flora. Alexanders, as has been noticed since the arrival of the first naturalist, William Turner in the sixteenth century, were "common about the island". The Peonies were coming into bud: "Noticed a clump under the Tower rock on a ledge of the cliff. Also a single plant about the old Inn."

His other observation, however, is from a very different island from that which will greet twenty-first century visitors. It must still have been grassy, with a herb-rich limestone turf, for him to note "Cowslips – very common, not yet in full flower".

Blathwayt speculated in 1906 that it might be on Steep Holm that the first Firecrest and Red-breasted Flycatcher would be spotted for the Somerset county list. For one he would be half-right, though by then it would have been recorded from the mainland, as in 1975-76 Firecrests visited the island and one was ringed.

Coastguard station

The desertion by the military of the Steep Holm Barracks came at a time when the spectre of shipwrecks again haunted the island. The Spanish barque *Anita* had gone down off Steep Holm, with all her crew, in 1901 and HM Coast Guard decided to have a permanent watchkeeper in the Barracks.

Charles Falconer Campbell, a Gaelic speaker from Thurso, was on Steep Holm for the Coast Guard service in the first years of this century. His wife broke her femur on the island. He left Steep Holm in 1908-09 and bought a newspaper shop in Penarth, where he used the name Charles Falconer.

Coast Guard service on the island may have been continued until after the Great War, but meanwhile Steep Holm would also have some tenants who actually stayed on the island.

Holmness of 'True Tilda'

As Steep Holm had come to the nineteenth century romantic imagination through William Lisle Bowles and his poem about the Wild Peony, then it would enter the libraries of the early twentieth century in an adventure story for children.

He caught up his oar and called to Tilda.

Frontispiece:
from 'True Tilda'.

True Tilda, by "Q" – Sir Arthur Quiller-Couch [1863-1944] – was published in 1909. Its other heroine is the island of Steep Holm, alias the uninhabited Holmness, to which the girl and boy row. The man of letters does not, unfortunately, give us much of a vignette of the island in Edwardian times. He has problems with his square measure, converting the 50 acres to a colossal 356 acres, in the description that an old man looks up for the children in the library:

"Extreme length, three-quarters of a mile; Width at narrowest point, 165 yards. It contains 356 acres, all of short grass, and affords pasturage in summer for a few sheep from the mainland. There is no harbour; but the south side affords fair anchorage for vessels sheltering from N.W. winds. The distance from nearest point of coast is 3¾ miles. Reputed to have served anciently as rendezvous for British pirates, and even in the last century as a smugglers entrepôt. Geological formation . . ."

Holmness swarms with rabbits and has gulls' eggs: "She had

not a notion how gulls' eggs tasted. Raw eggs! they would certainly be nasty; but raw eggs, after all, will support life. Moreover, deliverance might come, before long."

Tilda's companion, Arthur Miles, and 'Dolph' the dog, were then reunited. Their boat had vanished but they found a house on the island that was kept as a shelter for stranded seafarers. Arthur made the discovery: "Marmalade – real marmalade! And a spoon too – there are heaps of spoons and cups and glasses, and a fire ready laid. And – see here – biscuits!"

The next incident is the washing ashore, alive but dying, of "a noble stag" that had been hunted into the sea on the mainland.

Back there the children are pronounced missing and as part of the search Sir Miles Chandon, the island's owner, comes across in his steam launch from Fair Anchor Station on the Somerset coast. It is a rescue into the failing light: "Sunset lay broad and level across the Severn Sea, lighting its milky flood with splashes of purple, of lilac, of gold. The sun itself, as they approached the Island, dropped behind its crags, silhouetting them against a sky of palest blue."

Sleeman interlude

In 1909 James Sleeman and his 19-year-old son (also named James) came to the island to recover from tuberculosis. They were maltsters from Millend Mills, Eastington, Gloucestershire. They thought "the island life and sea air would do them good" and paid £30 a year to the Wharton estate. The rest of the family soon became entranced by Steep Holm and a sister, aunt and two other sons also moved to the island and made their home in the Barracks, living by farming and fishing. They kept a goat and a donkey.

Gradually the family drifted back to the mainland and when the younger James's health improved sufficiently, in 1912, he joined them. Their furniture and fishing and shooting tackle had been left in the Barracks.

One day when he was repairing the Barracks roof, James Sleeman looked up and saw an eagle overhead. There was some indecision over the species, which is understandable given that the Sleemans would claim the sighting as a White-tailed Eagle.

In the spring of 1914, word filtered through to Millend Mills that there had been a burglary on Steep Holm and the younger James landed with Pc Carter of Weston police to investigate. They found a different type of raider when they landed on 18 May 1914.

H.E. Landen, headmaster of Brynmelyn School at Coombe Road in Weston, had invaded the island for a botanical expedition with fifty of his pupils. Some of the boys were having joy-rides on the island's donkey and others were "carrying flowers in containers". Two of the island's three beds of Peony had been "wantonly damaged" and only the third, which was well-hidden, had escaped.

On a previous trip the same boys had swarmed over the cliffs and taken birds' eggs. As for the policeman, he had tea with Mr Landen and did not think the boys could do any damage "walking over the short grass". Sleeman, on the other hand, was furious, and successfully took out an injunction in Weston-super-Mare county court in July 1914 "restraining people from landing on the island without permission". He was awarded nominal damages of a shilling each against four Weston boat-men: John Baker, Henry Baker, W. Glover and Albert Counsell.

One aside at the hearing concerned the island's donkey and goat. An inspector for the National Society for the Prevention of Cruelty to Animals visited the island to see if there was sufficient food and water for the animals "but made no complaint about their condition".

For most of those fifty Brynmelyn boys, their next sailing was destined to be to a bigger confrontation. Several of them never returned from the trenches of the Western Front.

It may be from the Sleeman burglary that an apocryphal-sounding piece of Steep Holm folklore would arise. Their property that was left in the Barracks included, it is said, a set of the *Encyclopaedia Britannica*. When Edmund Mason first took us across to the island, in 1973, he told me about the fate of those volumes. The island was burgled and they were dropped one by one into the sea as the raiders made their escape from a pursuing craft. It was in response to this that Weston magistrates warned that trespassers to the island would face imprisonment "without the option of a fine", such must have been the empty state of our prisons in those good old days.

Another lingering association of the Sleemans and the island is that John Barrett's writings always talk of the steps beside Garden Battery East as "Sleeman's Steps". In fact, they are clearly depicted by the Ordnance Survey in its large-scale plan of 1883, though probably either Sleeman or his son rebuilt them; as I would between 1974-80, at the rate of one a year, until Chris Maslen started coming to the island and I could pretend not to notice their condition.

Birds shot

Steep Holm would not be fortified during the Great War of 1914-18 but its Coast Guard watch continued or was resumed. The single recorded casualty on the island during the First World War would be a male Corncrake, on the last St George's Day of the conflict.

That was on 23 April 1918. Mrs Evelyn Smith, who was living on the island and whose husband was probably in the Coast Guard, sent it to Dr J. Wiglesworth, of Winscombe, who had it stuffed for his collection. Wiglesworth had rowed out to the island and kept reminding the islanders to tell him about the rarer birds. These, then, included the Cormorant. "It is the sole breeding place in the county of the Cormorant," the doctor wrote.

Thomas Grills, one of the Coast Guards, wrote to Wiglesworth from "HM Coast Guard, Steepholme Island" on 23 July 1918: "In reply to your letter of the 18th re the Cormorants. I am quite positive the Cormorants did not nest on the Island this year. I kept all the north side of the island under close observation up to the present and there has been no sign of any young birds, the old birds have been here off and on apparently for feeding or passing in the direction of Breandown, sometimes the pair at other times singly.

"The Peregrine Falcon hatched out four young birds. The Wheatear that I mentioned to you disappeared early in June. I am afraid the Manx Shearwater does not nest here, as I have never heard it. No other birds noted only the usual residents. I will write to you later if I see any strangers when they migrate."

Colonel H.G. Lascelles was another distinguished Somerset birdman. In 1921 he was outraged to hear that a Welshman had shot a Peregrine, believed to be the Steep Holm breeding hen, on the island. Lascelles presented the information to the Royal Society for the Protection of Birds which prosecuted and obtained a conviction – with a ten shillings fine – and in 1922 the matter had also been resolved by the Steep Holm tiercel which had found a new mate.

World's first guided missile

The shape of man's aerial wars to come, in conflicts beyond 1939-45, roared across the water off Steep Holm in 1927. It was the world's first guided missile and it was British. In effect it was what we would call a ship-launched cruise missile. John

Pitfield has found me the facts.

It was fired from the deep water channel to the west of Rudder Rock and flew westwards down the length of the Bristol Channel towards the open sea. Apart from having a propeller it otherwise looked like a jet aircraft. This was the Larynx, which had been created by the Royal Aircraft Establishment at Farnborough. In 1925 the Air Ministry had issued a requirement for a Surface to Surface Missile (SSM) to carry a 200 lb warhead 200 miles in one hour. The project got under way the following year, under the description of the Remotely Piloted Vehicle (RPV), which became known as Larynx, the name being derived from the 220 hp Amstrong-Siddeley Lynx radial engine with which the machine was powered. The prototype made the hundred mile flight down the Bristol Channel after being launched from a destroyer, HMS *Stronghold*, by hydraulic catapult. It was guided by auto-pilot, with progress plotted by radio on shore and telemetry being used to transmit engine rpm. This long flight off the Somerset, Devon and Cornish coastline proved that remotely-controlled missiles were now a reality.

Testing of the missile moved on via Baghdad to the desert range of the RAF's Iraq Command. There it was armed with 250 lb of high explosive. George Gardner, who as Sir George Gardner would take charge of Farnborough in 1955, saw the project through to the usual point at which British inventions are shelved pending their adoption by other nations.

Thirties rediscovery

Leo Harrison Matthews had been a member of the *Discovery* expedition to the Antarctic in 1924. He found there an exceedingly unusual island which he described in 1931, in a book on *South Georgia: the Empire's Subantarctic Outpost*. A much smaller island, however, was to fascinate him all his life. For he had first visited Steep Holm, though he did not land, at the age of eight in 1909 when he went for a shilling motor-boat trip around the island from Weston.

"During the 1930s I was there several times, and stayed several nights each time," he recalled in a letter to Ernest Neal in 1978. "Harry Cox, who lived in a hut on Brean Down, was the tenant. In the winter of 1931-32 he fished the old hangs on the eastern spit and had two or three fishermen working for him there, but the venture did not pay and was not repeated.

"One of the men had a .303 rifle there, illegally, and it was left behind at the end of the fishing season. Somehow the police got to know of this and when I went over to the island on 28 May 1932, with Harry Cox, he was anxious to retrieve it. The fisherman said he had hidden it under the floor of the Barracks.

"We found a small access trap in the floor at the west end of the big room, and I squeezed through and crawled spread-eagled about on the earth and rubbish under the floor. I found the rifle, and a couple of clips of ammo – and also a moth-eaten pair of artillery uniform trousers (blue with a red stripe down each side), a copy of the Bristol Times and Mirror for 1897 full of the Diamond Jubilee celebrations, and a Coronation enamelled tin mug for Edward VII and Alexandra. Harry Cox had the rifle and newspaper, I had (still have) the coronation mug, and the trousers or what remains of them are probably still there."

Writing on Weston's "Channel Islands", in the *Weston-super-Mare Guide* for 1933, Harry Cox – who was leasing Steep Holm from the Wharton Estate – mentions the fishing: "The island is not inhabited at the moment except in the winter, when a few fishermen live here who are in the employ of the lessee. The fishing grounds adjacent are the best in this part of the Channel. Sprats, whiting, cod and skate are the principal catches."

Cox also mentions that the island "is covered with plant-life" and refers to what must be the sycamores above the eastern beach – "even large trees clothe some of the slope". The "northern side is precipitous and its cliffs are an imposing spectacle".

He goes on to call it "an island of history, mystery and romance" and proceeds to add disinformation to all three by claiming Gildas wrote his book on the island, that "Githa, the wife of King Harold sought refuge" there, and that "it is in the parish of Brean".

Fact emerges from fancy in a potted paragraph on the fauna, which confirms the ascendancy of the gulls, the continued breeding of the Raven and Peregrine, and the presence of many slow-worms:

"A thousand pairs of gulls nest on the Steep Holm, mainly herring and lesser black-backed, but there are a few pairs of greater black-backed too. Cormorants and sheldrake reside and nest here and so do raven and peregrine falcon. There are neither rats, mice nor snakes, but slow-worms – often thought to be snakes – are common."

The article ends by saying that the locations of the rare plants, such as the Wild Peony, Wild Leek and Bucksthorn Plantain, will only be revealed to naturalists who are being watched: "These plants will only be shown to botanists when in the company of the lessee – for it has been discovered that some botanists are unscrupulous, as are some ornithologists." The final twist is a neat turning round of William Lisle Bowles's verse about the island, not that Cox mentions this as the source, "on that great rock which after all, is neither barren nor forbidding even though it is lonely".

It was in August 1935 that as a special lecturer in zoology, for the University of Bristol, Harrison Matthews began to encourage Bristol Naturalists' Society into mounting a multi-discipline scientific investigation of the island. He also "did some digging in the ruins but did not find any antiquities of interest". The return to Steep Holm "for quite a jamboree" was in 1938. The official findings omit the following anecdote: "Camping out in the Barracks, we had no mirror, so I used to comb my hair looking at my reflection in the rainwater tank to the east of the Barracks. There was a lot of rat-tailed dipterous larvae at the bottom. The last morning I left the aluminium comb on the parapet and forgot to take it away. But it was still there when I was there about six months later – and I still have it."

"A Survey of Steep Holm" was published in the Proceedings of the Bristol Naturalists' Society in 1939 and was the largest corpus of material on the island until John Fowles and I compiled and edited *Steep Holm – a case history in the study of evolution* in 1978. That in turn has been expanded into the present series of books.

Hitler's War

The story of the massive Second World War re-fortification of Steep Holm island begins with a moment that is as ludicrous as any invented for the scripts of *Dad's Army*. The Weston-super-Mare company headquarters of the Local Defence Volunteers, before Winston Churchill had them re-named the Home Guard, decided to mount an invasion watch from Steep Holm. Three men were taken to the island along with a bicycle.

That was to be their means of communication – using pedal-power and its dynamo to flash messages in morse code to the mainland. One of their first such messages was an SOS. Boatman Frank Watts recalls that his father was sent across to remove the unit: "The isolation had got to them and one had flipped. He was completely off his rocker and we found him chasing the other two around the island, waving a gun and threatening to kill them."

The sequel is that Steep Holm would be occupied by the real Army in 1941, on the orders of Churchill's War Cabinet, but for an entirely different purpose. The threat of Operation Sealion and imminent invasion had passed and would be ended forever as the German Wehrmacht prepared three million men for Operation Barbarossa – the invasion of Russia.

Britain was looking the other way and preparing for an influx of heavy equipment, munitions and food from across the Atlantic. There was enough of a problem bringing the convoys across the U-boat infested ocean without facing the prospect of further losses, from E-boats or air attack, in home waters. Since the German occupation of France the Admiralty had been forced to close the English Channel to all but utterly essential shipping, and the series of ports along the Bristol Channel were therefore chosen as the safest option. Their principal problem was that the ships would have to lie at anchor for many hours whilst waiting the tide before entering port to unload. This difficulty was compounded by the fact that the convoy system brought ships into the ports in droves and therefore further waiting for a berth would also be inevitable.

The solution was to use the islands in the upper Bristol Channel as stone frigates and to link them with the headlands on both sides of the estuary to protect the proposed de-grouping

Operation Steep Holm: advance party of 930 Port Construction and Repair Company of the Royal Engineers land on the island's beach. Seen from the east, from the sea. Photographed by Albert Harden in July 1941.

areas, in the triangle between Barry, Steep Holm and Cardiff, from air or sea attack. These coast defence batteries were named the Fixed Defences, Severn, and the headquarters for the Commander was a concrete bunker at Swanbridge, which survives in a grove of trees opposite Sully Island, on the Welsh side. From it twenty-one telephone landlines went to coast defence batteries being built at Lavernock Point, and there were then a string of 65 mm insulated copper cables to be laid underwater to the islands of Flat Holm and Steep Holm and the headland of Brean Down on the English mainland. All three points were also to have coast defence batteries. Sixteen telephone lines would serve Steep Holm.

The regimental headquarters for the Fixed Defences, Severn, would be the pre-war Butlin's holiday camp at Nell's Point, Barry Island, which is now the Majestic holiday camp. Its first occupants were 531 Coast Regiment of the Royal Artillery, who would be succeeded by 570 Coast Regiment.

In 1976, with the help of Michael Yesson and a letter appealing for information which was published by the Daily Mirror – the officers who responded claimed only to have been told about it – I collected the experiences of those who had served on the island. Uncomfortable memories of the Steep Holm months were held by those who served on the island, and in particular amongst the men who carried out its initial re-fortification. The work was undertaken by 930 Port Construction and Repair Company of the Royal Engineers, formed in the spring of 1941 under the command of Major D.P. Bertlin.

S.G. Rock, who kept the company's war diary, described it as "a technical company with a high proportion of territorials and reserve personnel who, in peacetime, were engaged in the civil engineering industry, specialising in marine construction".

In 1941 they built jetties and fortifications at Steep Holm, Flat Holm, Brean Down, Drake's Island at Plymouth, and in the Clyde estuary. The work at Steep Holm began in July 1941 and was to last until October 1942. In the Bristol Channel operations the company was based at Barry Dock and Major Bertlin requisitioned a small coastal steamer of about 300 tons, the motor vessel *Assurity*, owned by Everards of Greenhithe and on charter to the War Department. She was unsuitable for laying moorings and another smaller motor barge from Greenwich, the motor vessel *Peter Piper*, was used, as she was fitted with a heavy derrick and dropped a large concrete block on to the bed of the Channel off Steep Holm. A chain was attached to the block at one end, and a steel floating buoy at the other. The buoy had a mooring shackle.

Operation Flat Holm: Assurity beached and steel girders being unloaded for Meccano-style construction of a V-trestle jetty by 930 Port Construction and Repair Company of the Royal Engineers. The same vessel and procedure were used to build the Steep Holm Pier. Seen from the north-west. Photographed by Harold Parr in July 1941.

Operation Steep Holm: barge beached at high-tide as construction begins of the V-trestle pier. A stone-built Quay would follow beside the cliff. Seen from the east from the stern of construction vessel Assurity. Photographed by Harold Parr in July 1941.

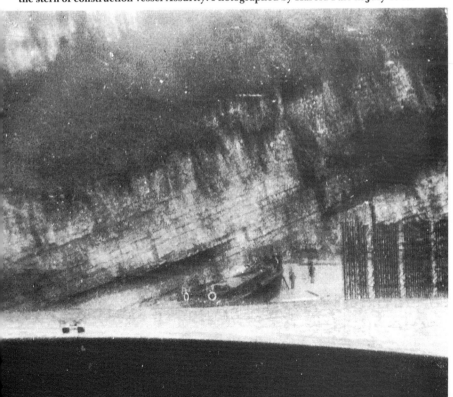

"Our task was to fortify the islands to repel any possible enemy force coming up the Bristol Channel," Major Bertlin recalled. " Because of the steep path to the top of Steep Holm, mules were landed on the beach by tank landing craft and I planned a zig-zag railway to haul the guns up the steep cliff. We also built a high-water jetty using standard military trestle-pier building units."

The footings of the wartime jetty were visible for a week in October 1976. The sea had scoured the beach of loose stones and exposed the smaller pebbles, firmly embedded in clay, which lie below. The jetty foundations – steel tubes set into concrete in two regular lines – ran due east from the 1941 beach-side stone wall, towards low water mark on the southern side of the spit, or 'cassey' as it is called by boatmen. Within days, gales and equinoctial flood tides swept hundreds of tons of stone back on to the beach, and its relics of the 1941 operation were hidden again beneath three feet of pebbles. By 1980 they were out of the water again and proving a danger to the island's ferry, as only a thin covering of brown Bristol Channel water would hide the projecting tangles of steel and concrete. These were blasted with gelignite by Mike Webber and a team from the Amey Roadstone Corporation's quarry at Batt's Combe, Cheddar, with the assistance of Neville Harrison of Explosives and Chemical Products Limited. They underestimated the extent and depth of the foundations which 930 Port Construction and Repair Company had laid for its pier.

The pier carried double railway lines, with a derrick and a generator at the quayside. This 1941-built quay wall still stands to 6 metres high and a length of 35 metres. The northern section of the wall, the recessed part, had a master-builder. It is built in snecked coursing that faithfully copies the grand style of the Victorian masonry that was demolished at Garden Battery, Tombstone Battery and Laboratory Battery in order to provide its ashlar blocks.

That northern section of the quay wall, Bert Harden remembered, was built upon a tilting section of bed-rock. This emerged from the pebbles and slanted up to a gate and a little footbridge across a chasm. I asked him if there were the foundations of the mediaeval monastic Gatehouse but he said the ledge was far too narrow for that; it only widened sufficiently for a building at the outcrop now occupied by the Inn. Lower down, Mr Harden said, would have been no place for a building, "as they would have had the sea in every week".

Two types of equipment were in use for jetty construction, known as L-type and V-type trestling, and it appears the former was used on Steep Holm beach. "Both were constructed on the 'Meccano' principle," Mr Rock said, "the steelwork being fabricated and pre-drilled for speedy erection and bolting under war conditions. Due to the tidal conditions in the Bristol Channel, the jetty was constructed so it dried out at low water. It was usable only around high water."

It had been built from the seaward end towards the land. *Assurity* was driven up the beach on the tide and the girders were removed on to the pebbles as the water ebbed. *Assurity* would be left high and dry till she refloated with the next tide.

Those who actually carried out the physical work remembered well, but without Mr Rock's enthusiasm for the technical details. "When we landed on Steep Holm, the only occupants were seagulls and the largest earwigs I have ever seen," said Harold Parr of Catford. "We were under canvas and although it was a sweltering summer we slept wearing Balaclava helmets to keep the monsters out of our hair. In the morning there was always a ball of earwigs, bigger than one's fist, up the top of the tent poles.

"Little time was lost over meals because we were only fed on bully-beef and biscuits. Breakfast was porridge made from biscuits, and we had no bread. If the boat was weather-bound in Barry we went without our ration of cigarettes and chocolate. Non-smokers sold their Woodbines at sixpence each. Conditions were bad, unnecessarily so."

This view was echoed by Bert Harden of Westcliff-on-Sea: "Building the jetty on Steep Holm and carving an approach road up the cliffs, along an old rabbit run, proved to be one of the hardest tasks we ever had to tackle and we had to be pushed to the limits of human endeavour in order to complete on schedule in the foulest conditions imaginable. We built our jetty and road on Steep Holm, as we did our other section on Flat Holm, at a cost of four men dead. Soon afterwards we were in Africa, and from there to Salerno and Anzio, followed by D-day in Normandy. What followed almost erased the memory of the starvation and misery of those days on Steep Holm, though our experience helped us to overcome everything we met later in the war.

"Despite recurring periods of near starvation and sickness, men worked from dawn to dusk every day and once a month we were allowed ashore for 48 hours for baths and medical inspection. I was doing a lot of diving and underwater work during one period and at low tide we would work waist-deep in water, causing cramp in my legs. I told the doctor, who advised me to have an occasional beneficial paddle in salt water. I'd done nothing else for weeks on end."

The problem with supplying Steep Holm was that stores had to be unloaded at high tide, when often a strong race runs across the east beach. *Asssurity* was only capable of about four knots and the tide off the tip of the island often moves at over six knots. "It needed nerves of steel to bring her close enough to unload stores," Mr Harden pointed out. "Many times she failed, and left us starving and desperate, returning to the mainland with everything we longed for.

"Our senior officers on the island were Captain 'Black' Morgan and Lieutenant Peter Hopper, a Canadian veteran from the First World War. He was dubbed 'Two-gun Pete' as he carried two low-slung revolvers strapped to his thighs. Once, when we had gone without proper food for at least ten days, and supplemented our rations with gull eggs, birds and rabbits, *Assurity* was standing off-shore in the lee of a gale, waiting for calmer waters in order to unload. After several attempts at coming in without being dashed against the cliffs the skipper – who was a relief man – informed us he was returning to Barry.

"At this, 'Two-gun Pete' whipped out a revolver and threatened to blow the skipper's head off if he didn't bring the ship in. Even that was to no avail, and we had to wait for our regular skipper to return two days later."

Mr Parr, a company lighterman, was involved in the carrying of supplies. The method of unloading in the early stages of the military occupation was to run in on to the beach as far as possible, and then throw all the steelwork overboard. This was retrieved when the water ebbed. The boat itself, after dropping its load of metal, had to be warped back a length on its stern anchor, and kept afloat whilst the rest of the cargo was ferried ashore in a couple of ships's lifeboats. After a time the *Peter Piper* was withdrawn, and the island men had the use of a Bristol dumb-barge, *Yumbi*, which was towed from Barry. Mr Parr was responsible for her: "I had to moor her, ground her, and then see that the aft-end of the barge was emptied before the tide came back – otherwise she wouldn't have lifted, lying as she did on such an angled, sloping beach."

It is Mr Parr who has solved the mystery of the island's wartime water supply. As Steep Holm never suffers any shortage of underground water, collected from roof run-off, it seemed inconceivable to be told that amongst all its other problems 930 Port Construction and Repair Company had to bring drinking water in four-gallon cans from Barry. Elaborate stage-tanks were constructed on concrete platforms, one beside the railway and the north end of Cliff Cottage, and another two on

Builders of wartime Steep Holm: 930 Port Construction and Repair Company of the Royal Engineers, en masse outside the west end of the Palmerstonian Barracks. One of their Nissen huts is glimpsed behind. Seen from the east, from the window of another Nissen hut. Photographed by C. Maddison in October 1941.

the top of the island to the south of the Ordnance Survey triangulation pillar.

The explanation, according to Mr Parr, is that the men were drinking water from the island's main water-tank behind the Barracks, or alternatively from the ancient cliff-side Monks' Well, which was rebuilt and given an iron lid. There was then some sickness and typhoid was suspected. To arrive on the island it would have needed a carrier, but Steep Holm's 'navvies' included men from the Indian Army, a part of Asia where the disease was endemic. "One lad was very bad," Mr Parr said. "The weather was stormy at the time and the only boat that got through to us was a launch, which was for officers only. Another day went by before our motor barge arrived to take the sick man ashore.

"He died in the ambulance on his way to hospital in Barry. The well was investigated and found to contain typhoid bacteria. It had become polluted as the latrines had seeped through into it. This was not rectified while we were on the island, and all our water from then on came from the mainland in cans. It became as scarce as food and for washing we were rationed to one bowl for twelve men. If you were on cementwork and were at the end of the queue, it wasn't very successful. Towards the latter part of our stay they sent us some salt-water soap. That was like trying to get a lather from a pebble off the beach."

Other casualties were caused by accidents. Three men, newly posted to Major Bertlin's team, drowned off Flat Holm: "We very tragically lost three men when the Navy, at my request, attempted to land at Flat Holm. They were put into a dinghy with the idea that they should be rowed ashore.

"The dinghy collapsed and all three men were immediately drowned as they were encumbered by military equipment. The seaman rowing them, being without equipment, was saved. My officer, Hopper, awaiting them on the shore, was powerless to to anything to help."

On Steep Holm two sepoys of the Royal Indian Army Service Corps, in charge of a mule team, died on the island. Thomas Naughton, of 930 Port Construction Company, told of German bombers dropping sea-mines into the Bristol Channel shipping lanes: "One sea-mine dropped on the island one night, before we had finished building the jetty. I was the only one hurt, with a brick and flying glass. We were playing cards by candlelight at the time, and I finished up in the RAF hospital near Barry. There were only twelve of us on the island then." S.G. Rock, too, remembers the mines: "My own recollection of the period was of frequent nightly visits of German aircraft, which mined the approaches to Cardiff and Barry, and of the floating mines which were daily swept and detonated around the island, causing the gulls to ascend in white clouds from Steep Holm. I also remember that our soldiers used to supplement their army rations with the fishy-tasting gulls' eggs collected from the cliffs."

For W.G.M. Jones as well, on the island in 1943, the gulls are remembered for their contribution to the war effort: "They seemed to appear on the same day towards the end of February. One day there were none – the next day the island was covered with them. They were laying all over the island during April and although one tried to preserve the greater part of Steep Holm as a bird sanctuary this was not at all popular with the men, who reckoned to augment their low pay by selling the eggs. To have adopted a rigid attitude in the matter would have caused a great deal of ill-will. The men gathered the eggs and sold them to an NCO for one penny each. He sold them to the man on the boat for twopence. He sold them to the shops in Barry for threepence and the shopkeepers sold them for four-pence each. The eggs were palatable hard-boiled or fried. One man going down the cliff after eggs nearly lost his life in March 1943. I learned later that the rope had broken and there was great difficulty getting him up again. This happened near the searchlight at Rudder Rock."

G.A. King presented a summary of the state of the island's defences at the end of Major Bertlin's work: "The company of Royal Engineers laid a railway around the island for transporting stores and shells. They also built the iron jetty, and cut a three-tier trackway to the top of the island. A donkey engine was placed in a winch-house at the top of each one of these three cuts, to pull up the skips on railway lines. Gun emplacements were built at what we called the 'South' and 'Garden' ends of Steep Holm. We, that's myself and twelve other gunners of the Royal Artillery under a Battery Sergeant Major, put the six-inch coast defence guns in, and we also had two machine guns for air defence. There was also a troop of the Royal Indian Army Service Corps, with mules, under a King's Corporal."

There have also been references to Indians of the Pioneer Corps working on the building of the island's cliff-side railway, but the documents I have seen mention only the Royal Indian Army Service Corps as having, as one would expect, non-British personnel. The railway that was installed has a gauge of 60 cm

Feldbahn: captured from the Germans in the Great War and put in store for use against them in the next European conflict. Relaid on the cliffs of Steep Holm in 1941. Converted to an incline system with the addition of British-made winches and cable-wheels (left: by A.C.E. Machinery Limited of London). Seen from the north. Photographed by Colin Graham in 1983.

(1 foot 11½ inches). Or rather it has a "Spurweite" because it is German, built for the Wehrmacht as a "Feldbahn", a field railway, on the Western Front where it was captured – after a great blood letting on both sides – by the British Army in 1916-18. Sections were put in store at Rochester and on the Longmoor Military Railway. It was never intended to operate on an incline and the Royal Engineers on Steep Holm had to bend the profile of the rails in several places, with oxyacetylene torches, and add fittings such as cable-wheels and rail-switching levers, so that it could operate up the eastern slope with winches to provide electrical and manual traction up the zig-zag of three inclines.

The wagons seem to have been metal-framed German trucks rather than the ordinary wooden type then found in West Country mineral workings. These trucks carried 406 kilos in normal operation but because of the slope there was a weight-limit and there may also have been a safety rule that only one truck could be winched at a time. Railway historians have traced the dispersal of 70 kilometres of German field railway that had been brought home by the British but the 500 metres on Steep Holm comprise most of what survives. This figure includes the other section of rails in the steeper incline down to the South Landing. There would have been a similar length in use on top of the island but that was removed after the war. Mules provided the motive power on the level sections of line, which operated as a horse-drawn tramway, and there are a selection of their shoes in a display case at the Barracks.

The first parties of sappers staked out their sleeping quarters in the Victorian Barracks on the top of the island. Leslie R. James of 930 Port Construction and Repair Company would never forget his first night on the island in July 1941. "Jock and I slept in a small room at the end of the building," he said. "We lay on a trap-door with a ring in it". This is still in place, in the north-west corner of the main West Dormitory. "Going to bed footsteps were heard, the door opened, footsteps again, the trap-door raised with us on it and bumped down. No one was seen."

Others left their physical marks. There is a pencilled graffito on the east wall of the East Dormitory: "SAPPER GIBBONS 1941 ROYAL ENGINEERS 930 PORT CONSTRUCTION AND RE-PAIR COMPANY". A little of their wet cement was used to improve the domestic situation and the inscription is in the north-west corner of the concrete floor in the East Dormitory: "L CHARLTON 1941 R Es".

The sea-facing line of Barracks windows were partially

blocked, to a metre high, with blast-walls to lessen the risk of eye-level glass and bullets from aerial strafing. These emergency walls, built as with other war-works with materials from the Welsh side of the water – the Star Brick Company of Caerleon – remain in place and have obliterated the building's pre-war view of Bridgwater Bay and the west Somerset coast. Along the northern walls of the building, where there is almost complete protection from the Victorian-blasted rock face that rises to roof level, the windows were left to their full seat-level depth.

Three superb wartime touches survive in the Barracks. My admiration goes to the craftsman who rose beyond austerity concrete when he roofed the 6.5 metre gap between the west and east wings of the building. He finished off his steel and concrete beams with the stylish chamfers he would have brought to timbers of fine oak. The other unexpected relics, which visitors do note and appreciate, are the "Durbanian" (by Micklethwait of Rotherham) and "Bulwark" (by Lane and Girvan of Bonnybridge) – the big Victorian cast-iron stoves which cannot fail to impress.

Naafi cups and officers' plates include one of the latter that is stamped "G VI R 1943" for "George Sixth Rex" and the cups, which are much more plentiful, include standard issues which just carry the Naafi initials and the date, either 1941 or 1942. Examples are displayed in the archaeological cabinets in the Barracks.

On the top of the island, Major Bertlin's priority in October 1941 was the completion of four massive concrete casements to protect the guns that were being deployed on the island. These structures were to a basic design, adapted to suit the topography, that had a single 6-inch naval gun mounted centrally on a concrete platform, with a holdfast plate set into a metre diameter circle that was made up of eighteen 42 mm bolts. Behind it there was a flight of concrete steps down 1.22 metres to a lower concrete floor that had fourteen shell and cartridge lockers, each 1.1 metre wide by a metre deep, that had been brought out of store and were First World War vintage. Behind them and also at the sides was a protective blast-wall 71 cm thick, extending to 17 metres in width and 10 metres in depth.

The chosen locations were at the Victorian Garden Battery, to overlook Bridgwater Bay from the south-east corner of the island, and at Summit Battery, on the northern perimeter path, where the uninterrupted view is across the shipping lanes to Lavernock Point and Flat Holm. Each site was to have two guns, in separate casements, with these being offset from each other to improve upon the 190 degree traverse arcs their guns would otherwise have had. At Garden Battery this is a combined 250 degree field of fire and at Summit Battery the guns had a sweep of 260 degrees. They were built for anti-ship guns to protect the convoy de-grouping area against E-boat incursions.

Among the first Royal Artillerymen to arrive on the island in 1941 was one who left his mark on the western Victorian cannon at Summit Battery. He went to some trouble to etch: "EDWARD COX RA, 1941."

Each of the four concrete batteries deployed a 6-inch naval gun, of type O.B.L. Mark VII or Mark XI, that was manually operated and percussion fired. All had come from former warships or armed merchant vessels of the Great War and were brought to Steep Holm from the Armament Supply Depôt at Cardiff. They were "Transferred to Army Charge" by Armament Supply document AS 4213/46 of 29 September 1941 (though one gun, number 1815, was already Army property) and issued to the Officer Commanding Fixed Defences, Severn, for shipment to Steep Holm. The past history of each gun has been documented for us by military historian N.J.M. Campbell of the Isle of Wight.

Gun 1104: Made at the Royal Gun Factory (Woolwich) 1901, and issued for installation aboard the battleship HMS *Venerable*. Moved to armoured cruiser *Edinburgh Castle*, 1918. Stored at Bull Point, Plymouth, 1919-39. Put on armed merchantman *Ausonia*, 1939, then taken to Armament Supply Depôt at Cardiff on 3 September 1941.

Gun 1783: Made by Elswick Ordnance Co Ltd for Armstrong Whitworth, who fitted it to the armoured cruiser *Donegal*, in 1903. Stored at Chatham, 1919-41. Released to the Armament Supply Depôt, Cardiff, on 5 September 1941.

Gun 1815: Made by Vickers and Son Maxim, 1903, and used at Devonport Gunnery School. Fitted in 1916 to the armoured merchant cruiser *Kildonan Castle*. Taken off at Woolwich in 1918 and put in store at Chatham, 1919-41. Released to the Armament Supply Depôt, Cardiff, on 5 September 1941. Technically, this gun did not require a transfer document from Royal Navy to Army charge; it was already Army property.

Gun 2054: Made at the Royal Gun Factory (Woolwich) about 1903. Fitted by Vickers and Son Maxim to the battleship *Dominion* in 1904. Removed and put in store at Chatham in 1922. Released to the Armament Supply Depôt, Cardiff, on 5 September 1941.

Though they were from 29 September 1941 in Army charge, three of the four Steep Holm guns remained the property of the Royal Navy. It was only after they had been taken off the island that they were formally transferred to the Army in 1946.

Gunner Cyril Stickland, who was born in Charlton Mackrell, Somerset, in 1912 and retired to Seavale Road, Clevedon, would never forget his thirteen days on Steep Holm in October 1941. He told nextdoor neighbour Brian Chislett, an Auxiliary Coast-guard who is a member of the island's present-day work-force, that twenty-four members of 366 Coast Defence Battery of the Royal Artillery, from Queen's Dock, Cardiff, were sent to do "jankers on hard tack", in other words punishment on dried rations.

"It was worse than on D-Day," Stickland remembered. The four 6-inch naval guns had been delivered by barge from Card-fiff and 366 Battery was given the task of hauling them up to the top of the island. At the beach jetty the guns were prepared for the lifting operation. They had been stripped into eight parts with the "piece" – the gun barrel – having been separated from its "cradle" – the mounting. Each of the eight parts weighed around seven tons.

The gun barrels were put on the rails with bogie wheels being attached at each end. Being much more squat, however, the mountings required only a single bogie each. That part of the operation was achieved using a tripod and the gun parts were then winched up the newly constructed cliff railway.

Though the Royal Engineers and their Pioneer Corps navvies worked during the day the Royal Artillerymen could only move the guns at night. That was through fear of attracting the attention of the Luftwaffe, and even in the dark there was still concern about the possibility of air attack:

"We had no lights and would not have dared to use any for fear of being spotted from the air. When Jerry aircraft were known to be on the way we received a telephone warning and stopped work. We weren't even allowed to look up – a dozen white faces, they can see you, mind.

"One night, winching up a cradle" – the mounting for the gun barrel – "three-quarters of the way up the middle incline of the railway, before the second layby where it changes direction again, the hawser snagged under the track. The men on the winch stopped winding.

"We called for the two gun buckers" – experts in gun moving – "and they erected a tripod on the cliff edge. They were a joy to watch. They would pick up seven tons like you handle a pen. Here, though, that was with more trouble than usual as it was very narrow at that point. Using block and tackle they hoisted the cradle and eased the bogie back on to the track."

The rails bend gently but noticeably upwards and leftwards at the point of this mishap. If there was any surprise it was that the other seven sections were raised without derailment.

Their installation in the batteries was carried out in the first week of October 1941 by the "Repository" team from the School of Artillery at Llandudno. For at least the rest of the month, Major Bertlin continued to construct the casements behind them, with the Pioneer Corps doing most of the hard graft..

An added feature was a carapace of 'H'-profile steel girders, 128 mm by 155 mm in section, which was put over the rear of the emplacements – landward of the guns – as a flak-top. Another teutonic phrase was used at the time for that style of warfare, such were the German efforts at enriching our language; they were intended as protection against aerial strafing. *"Gott strafe England"*, was a cry of the German jingoes – "May God strafe England".

The carapace stood at a height of 2.4 metres above the floor of the gun platform and was raised 23 cm above the concrete wall of each emplacement. It also overhung these walls to give added protection. The gap between the girders and the wall was to allow it to buckle under impact without splitting the walls apart.

Joan Rendell was told these roofs were added as an afterthought: "The engineer in charge of building the flak tops for the emplacement, Corporal Graddon, told us they were an afterthought to protect against machine gun fire. They were erected in one day and no one had much faith in them. Practice firings were made to make sure the roof was not brought down."

I put the statement that they were a day's work to another Royal Engineer who was revisiting Steep Holm. He did some mental arithmetic of the sort that characterised the pre-calculator generation and muttered about so many hundred girders and fifty tons of steel plates and plastic armour. "Some people have shorter memories than others," he remarked.

That plastic armour was a 70 mm thick mastic of bituminous cement and flint and granite chippings that was poured on to the roof to set in squares between the latticework of the girders. At the bottom of each slab was a 1 metre square plate of 18 mm steel. This was a cheap alternative to armour plating that had been devised in August 1940. It absorbed armour-piercing rounds without shattering and was welcomed by Portsmouth Naval Gunnery Establishment as being "very greatly superior to any other non-magnetic material, excluding non-magnetic bullet-proof steel, so far tried ... it is most strongly recommended that the fitting of concrete protection should be discontinued and that Plastic Armour be fitted in its place". The problem with the standard concrete and steel canopies was that they shattered under aircraft cannon-fire. Plastic armour would save the Allies immense quantities of steel, and it was versatile enough to be used at sea, being fitted to some ten thousand ships.

As for carapaces of girders and their armoured roofs, these saw out the war on Steep Holm unscathed, but by 1984 they were disintegrating and sagging dangerously. Operations for their removal, with much more difficulty than anticipated, were carried out by the Amey Roadstone Corporation using traditional blasting techniques, and then by the Royal Ordnance Factory, Puriton, with their latest plastic Demex (*Demolition Explosive*). Everyone was impressed with the strength of the wartime steelwork and the slabs of plastic armour also came down substantially intact.

Garden Battery West: showing the grid of one metre squares of plastic armour that protected the steel canopies above the 1941-built 6-inch gun emplacements, and the generator house that powered the southern searchlights (right of centre, behind). Seen from the east. Photographed by Colin Graham in 1976.

Summit Battery East: showing ring of bolts for mounting its 6-inch naval gun, which would have been positioned midway between the figure and the girders supporting the flak-top that protected gunners and the cartridge store from strafing. Built in 1941 and surrounded by Alexanders in flower. Seen from the west. Photographed by Colin Graham in 1983.

Garden Battery West: inside the emplacement, built in 1941, showing vertical girders supporting the lattice of horizontal steelwork holding metre-square slabs of plastic-armour for the roof. Below, recessed into the concrete walls at floor level, are the armoured doors of the shell cupboards. Seen from the east. Photographed by Colin Graham in 1976.

Generator house: built in 1941, just east of Summit Battery, to power the northern and western searchlights. Seen from the west. Photographed by Colin Graham in 1976.

OVERLEAF, FIRST DOUBLE-PAGE SPREAD – **Air reconnaissance: the Pier on the beach (at low water) and the Royal Engineers building Garden Battery East at the top of the cliff. Note the lines of Nissen huts along the northern cliffs. Seen from the north-east. Photographed for Major D. P. Bertlin in September 1941.**

SECOND DOUBLE-PAGE SPREAD – **Air reconnaissance: fortification begins on the north cliffs. Work has started on the footings for Summit Battery West (right of centre) and there is a tent at Rudder Rock (lower right). Seen from the north-west. Photographed for Major D. P. Bertlin in September 1941.**

THIRD DOUBLE-PAGE SPREAD – **Air reconnaissance: Nissen huts can be glimpsed to the west of the Barracks (centre right) and in the Victorian cutting behind the Palmerstonian Split Rock Battery (left of lower wing-tip). A pipe-line crosses the top of the island. White concrete shows at Garden Battery East (below the top wing-tip). Seen from the south-west. Photographed for Major D.P. Bertlin in September 1941.**

89

Demex: smoke and powdered rust fill the sky as a team from the Royal Ordnance Factory, Puriton, demolish the roof of Summit Battery East with plastic explosives. The Generator House in the foreground was undamaged. Seen from the east. Photographed by John Stickland in 1986.

Half-down: the flak-top of Garden Battery East buckled and with its metre-squares of plastic armour shaken off by dozens of controlled explosions. Seen from the west. Photographed by John Stickland in 1986.

Garden Battery East: roof demolition progressing, after blasting, at the hands of a party of Venture Scouts. Island warden Rodney Legg is at the right (£5 note in hand, having just intercepted visiting yachtsmen). Seen from the north-west. Photographed by Colin Graham in 1985.

As for relics more directly associated with the guns, I have a 6-inch armour-piercing shell, which though not actually from the island was obtained via one of my Royal Artillery informants and delivered to Len Martin in Christchurch Road, Bournemouth, who was less than amused at its weight. On the island itself, on the scree slope below the Barracks in 1983, I found a brass gun-cleaner, stamped "C & S 6-INCH 1941", which is cylindrical with wooden rollers inset with bristles. It has obviously seen some use and has a dark green patina. "It's a brush piasaba," Bob Moon of Woodspring District Council told me in 1990, with the inference that everyone knows that, which may well be the case.

Gun-laying: brick blast-wall above Summit Battery East protects a concrete pillar on which Royal Artillery spotters positioned a Depression Range-Finder. Seen from the north-west. Photographed by John Pitfield in 1988.

Still surviving on the island are the two instrument pillars on which the Royal Artillery spotters mounted their DRFs. These were Watkin Depression Range-Finders, which were used to observe targets and correct the fall of fire, and they were regarded as being much superior to the Royal Navy's Barr and Stroud optical instruments. It was crucial, however, that they were levelled accurately, and this on Steep Holm meant resetting every half-an-hour to cope with the rise and fall of the tide.

One of the pillars is perfectly preserved and still has its protecting semi-circular shield of brickwork. It stands at 77 metres above sea-level, overlooking Summit Battery, with a sweep of 330 degrees that includes clear views of the shipping lanes and out to the open sea. The other pillar, without any blast-wall and now out of position, is at Garden Battery East, beside the surviving western Victorian barbette. Both were erected in August 1941 as a prerequisite to the installation of the guns.

Another essential was the provision of generator houses, to power the island's four searchlight posts, and for domestic lighting and ancillary duties. Diesel generators operated winches on the three inclines of the eastern cliff railway. Of those duties, the first was of primary importance to an island at war.

Any E-boat activity this far into British waters would have been most likely at night. Four searchlight posts were therefore provided for the Steep Holm gunners. Two are at the South Landing and above Calf Rock, built to a standard design that was 3 metres wide by 5 metres deep in reinforced concrete and with a projecting semi-circular front that is 2.5 metres high. The light was protected behind curved armoured steel shutters that were pulled back along brass rollers. Similar in design but not in terrain were two searchlights that were needed for the Summit Battery gunners on the northern cliffs. Here the precipitous cliffs were the obstacle.

The top of the island was far too high for the lights, as the angle would have been far too steep for them to pan the sea in an emergency, and they had to be constructed on ledges two thirds of the way down the side of the cliffs. The two chosen spots, where only nesting birds had ever set foot before, were at Rudder Rock, above the rock-arches on the western tip of the island, and at an even less accessible point 150 metres north-east of Summit Battery. The first required a flight of 120 steps and the second a far more awesome 208 steps to get the attendant from his light, at the side of a ninety foot sheer rock-face, back up to the island plateau. Towards the top the builders gave up trying to follow the clefts in the cliff and instead took to the air with a section that rises like a flying buttress on the side of a church. As with the gun batteries they would be painted with zebra-camouflage to help the flights of steps merge with the island cliffs.

Ray Howard Jones, an official war artist, visited Steep Holm in 1943. His watercolour of the "Searchlight Emplacement Coast Defence" at Rudder Rock shows the zebra-camouflage splashed not only across the wartime concrete but over the cliff-face as well. The canvas is in store in Bristol Museum, having been given to them by the Imperial War Museum, but all trace of the actual paint has long ago been washed by the elements from the Rock, though black streaks are visible at Garden Battery.

The purpose of the searchlights, and how they operated, was spelt out to me by Major David Benger, the staff officer of the Severn Fixed Defences, who corrected an erroneous suggestion that the island searchlights might have been used in pairs for geometrical range-finding: "Searchlight beams were not used by triangulation for calculating ranges, though given time to do it this would have been possible. The fact is that given fast-moving targets like E-boats at close range, the only thing possible was locating them by searchlight and then engaging them over open sights."

Major Benger also dismissed a report that the Royal Electrical and Mechanical Engineers had installed radar control equipment for the searchlights in 1942, which was before he arrived on the island. "There was no radar on Steep Holm," he said, "I think there may have been some misinterpretation of information here. I suspect that what was fitted in 1942 by REME was the standard Coast Artillery automatic control of searchlights from the Observation Posts. Lights could then be automatically traversed, elevated and depressed from the Command Post, and all the attendant at the Light had to do was stop and start generators, open and close shutters, expose and douse the light, and change carbons."

In 1942, when he arrived on the island, W.G.M. Jones found that all four of the 6-inch anti-ship guns were emplaced: "There were two batteries of two 6-inch guns each. The garrison was about 120". This needs re-stating because of a statement, or rather a supposition, that was made to me in 1976, to the effect that only one of each pair of batteries ever had a gun. "Quite certainly all four guns *were* emplaced," said Major Benger, who was the staff officer responsible for them in 1943-44, at the headquarters of the Commander Fixed Defences, Severn. He had come to the island as an exceedingly able young man, who had shot up through the ranks, and certainly knew how many guns he had with which to play the game.

The South Landing was provided with a stone jetty for use at times when the north to north-east winds made the use of the main pier impossible. The upper part of the South Landing jetty has the date "March 1942" inscribed in its wet cement. An exceedingly steep incline railway was laid to the top of the island where a manually operated winch was set into a recess which the Victorians had constructed for the same purpose, in their case to haul carts up from the Limekiln. The drum and casings of the Second World War winch survive, though the two cog wheels, gear-train and other fittings have been stripped.

The Barracks was taken over as offices and a mess and the overspill was housed in a complex of Nissen huts to the west of the main block. A displaced door at the Barracks still has the stencilling of the Officer Commanding: "O.C. 188 COAST BTY R.A." Another concentration of twenty-two concrete hut pads sprawls across the north-east corner of the island west of Laboratory Battery. The iron debris on the ground includes rusting hoops, curved roofing sheets of corrugated iron, and pieces of their "tortoise" stoves. The huts were invented by British engineer Peter Norman Nissen [1871-1930] which is why they do not have a Japanese spelling. North of the Priory ruin, at the head of the zig-zag railway, the ground is black with dust from the island's wartime coal dump. The Victorian Tombstone Battery became the island's sand pit.

A Scotsman, Bill Hunter of Kilmacolm in Renfrewshire, spent the summer of 1942 on Steep Holm as a 2nd Lieutenant with a gun crew at Summit Battery. The island was serviced from Barry with 570 Coast Regiment of the Royal Artillery operating all fixed gun positions in the upper Bristol Channel, including Barry, Brean Down, Cardiff, Flat Holm, Newport, Penarth, Portishead and Steep Holm. The main armament of 6-inch naval guns had an anti-ship role and practised on a large wooden target, the size of a motor boat, which was hauled by one of the regiment's support craft. Bill Hunter recalled: "On Steep Holm you had a great height and could appreciate the distance between the fall of shot. From 250 feet on the cliffs you are far more effective than firing at sea-level. You got on to the target quicker.

"Our function was coastal defence pure and simple. At Rudder Rock we had the Battery Observation Post. Below was one of the searchlights. These searchlight points had to be near the water to give the maximum effect. If they were higher up they would have been more like a spotlight. From the bottom of the cliffs they could silhouette any boats and cover a wide area of sea. In fact we could light up the entire Channel. The enemy never came. They must have known how prepared we were."

Mr Hunter's Steep Holm summer ended when he was removed in the island's supply vessel, suffering acute sciatica, on a rough day. He then endured seasickness as well. Whilst he was stationed in the Bristol Channel, Bill Hunter arranged for the D'Oyly Carte opera company, on tour at Cardiff, to perform to the gunners on Flat Holm. Their operatic songs were interspersed with light-hearted skits parodying themselves. "The foghorn was going all the time this was happening," Mr Hunter remembered.

Some graffiti from the Second World war survive underground on Steep Holm in a Victorian gun battery. The northern of the two chambers at Rudder Rock has red-painted writing on one of its walls: "189 BTY, AA, GNRS W. COLLINS, T. BONNER, J. HEARSLEY, F. GREEN, W. DULY." Major Benger recalled: "Lance-Bombadier Bonner was a master-plasterer, and he plastered out my command post on Flat Holm when it was built. Even today there is not a crack in the plaster." Above, in the same paint, the letters "RIP" have been added as an afterthought. Below, in smaller black lettering, is a similar note: "RA, 11 December 1941, 189 COAST BATTERY, GNRS LAVER R.R., AVERY H.F., BISHOP G.S.W., FRANCE P." From these it is clear that 189 Coast Battery of the Royal Artillery was garrisoning Steep Holm in 1941. The letters "AA" stand for Anti-Aircraft. At least six anti-aircraft gun mountings are on the island.

They were remembered for me by H. Shaw, a lecturer at Princess Marina College, Arborfield, Berkshire, who confirmed that the flat pads of concrete had each emplaced a Bofors Mark II 40 mm gun in a static position. "I was in 9 Anti-Aircraft Division's workshop in 1941-42," he said. His visits to Steep Holm and Flat Holm were to work on the generator sets. Flat Holm had 4.5 inch Heavy AA guns, to help protect Cardiff against bombers, and 40 mm guns against fighter-bomber attack. Steep Holm had 40 mm guns only. "The two islands were supplied by a Gosport ferry steam launch, would you believe, suitably armed and armoured," Mr Shaw said. "It still had its original crew who had sailed it round from Pompey."

David Benger confirmed that she was the *Princessa*, and was indeed the Gosport ferry, and proceeded to list the craft that were at his disposal.

The islands of Steep Holm and Flat Holm were both supplied from Barry Docks by a Water Transport Company of the Royal

Army Service Corps. They operated the following fleet of vessels, which were manned with civilian crews, in 1943-44:

Peter Piper and *Snowflake*. "These were two diesel-powered barges," recalled Major Benger, staff officer of the Severn Fixed Defences. "They were specially fitted-out for the job, the main modification being the fitting of large fresh-water tanks and a pump. *Peter Piper* was the larger. *Snowflake* had an odd-shaped bow, curving back at the top, and was said to have been built for the Dardanelles, the Gallipoli campaign of the First World War. In the mid-1980s I saw somewhere that there were still some of her class carrying sand and gravel in the Thames estuary, perhaps even *Snowflake* herself."

Vailima and *Corrieghoil*. "These were two luxury motor-yachts used for visits by VIPs," Major Benger said. "If the name *Vailima* sounds familiar, it was Robert Louis Stevenson's estate in Samoa."

Princessa. "This was the Gosport ferryboat," Major Benger said. "She was of very shallow draught, and very unstable in any sea. Once she shed her screw off Flat Holm while conveying most of the top brass of Western Command, who had to be rescued by a tug. A pity – there might have been a lot of promotion!"

Skipjack and *Margaret*. "These were two small motor-boats. They were converted to ships' lifeboats as far as I recall."

An occasional visitor to the Bristol Channel was the War Department steam-tug *Haslar*. She towed the targets for anti-ship gunnery practice, to exercise the 6-inch naval guns, and steamed around the islands.

Other occasional visitors were troupes from ENSA, the acronym of the Entertainments National Service Association – or "Every Night Something Awful" as wartime returnees insist – who came to break the isolation of one of Britain's more monotonous postings. Miss Edith Shute of Grangetown, Cardiff, told me that she was on the island for the Whitsun bank holiday of 1942: "I was the hostess in the officers' mess with an ENSA party organised by Mrs Charles of Cardiff. We stayed the night. There were six or seven girls and the same number of men, from Barry with the Naafi managers. We used your main room for the concert. It was the Naafi." This was the multi-purpose Barracks, which was no longer necessary for sleeping accommodation but now had offices and as its mess-room the open-plan main hall which was run by the Naafi (acronym of the Navy, Army and Air Force Institutes).

Another visit was to re-supply the island during something of a lull in a rough sea: "We came out another time just for the day

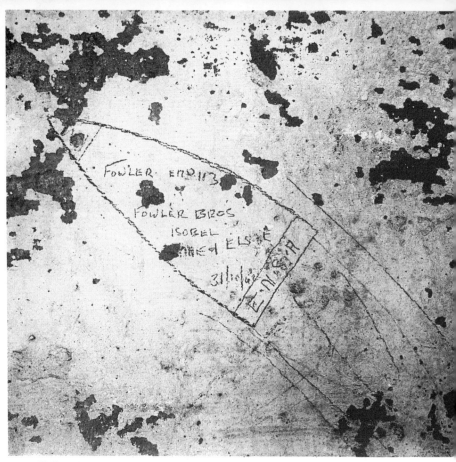

Hallowe'en to remember: graffito from an ENSA visit to Steep Holm in 1942, pencilled on the plaster of a wall in the eastern section of the Palmerstonian Barracks. Seen from the south. Photographed by Colin Graham in 1984.

and had to get off quick because the weather was beating-up. They had been cut off for a period of eight days. There were two hundred men here at the time. We went to Brean Down and picked up an officer there, and another at Flat Holm. It was the same journey going back and some people were horribly sick, though it was nice weather all the time."

Pencilling on the wall of the south-west room in the east part of the Barracks is in a shell-shaped surround and records a Hallowe'en ENSA visit: "FOWLER BROS, ISOBEL, ANNE & ELSIE. 31/10/42. ENSA." It may have been on this trip that the girls were stranded by worsening weather, which was no doubt welcomed by the battery's officers. I traced Elsie, who had become Mrs Elsie Parker Jones, to Penarth She remembered being marooned on Steep Holm by the weather. W.G.M. Jones, looking back to 1942-43, recalled that another of the ENSA girls was Betty Hardcastle, who lived in Weston-super-Mare.

In November 1942 a pig-sty was built as an extension to the north side of Cliff Cottage. It has a graffito, in concrete: "BUILT BY 189 COAST BATTERY R.A. – T.E.B., A.H.H. and A.H., C.W.A. NOV 1942." Mr Jones remembered that "somewhere near the wall was a pig-sty which was repaired and in which we kept some piglets on the swill".

It is disappointing that this account has to be patched together from random reminiscing, albeit with the aid of the diaries of Major Bertlin who transformed the rock into a war-machine, and Major Benger who saw it through to "Care and Maintenance" by the end of 1943 and decommission in 1944. The lack of a fuller account, with precise dates and times, is because the Ministry of Defence has been unable to find the exceedingly large volume that was the Steep Holm Fort Record Book from July 1941 when 930 Port Construction Company and the advance unit from the Royal Artillery arrived to fortify the island. Brean Down had a similar book which is also lost. That for Flat Holm has proved to be the fortunate exception and is now in the Public Record Office (reference WO 192, Fort Record Book class).

There would be all sorts of incidents recorded. One attendant of the 208 Steps searchlight is said to have failed to take a turn in the staircase at night and slipped under the hand-rail and slithered to his death on the rocks below. Another story is that in about 1942 a German raider dropped a parachute mine that exploded close to the caves at the north-east corner of the island and left scorch marks on the cliffs. These black smudges were apparently still visible after the war. The Fort Record Book would anchor memories to the facts and guard against the vague and folksy misinformation that masqueraded as the island's wartime history until I put the first detailed, and largely accurate, account into the 1978 publication *Steep Holm – a case study in the history of evolution*.

Memories of ENSA and the pigs have come to characterise the Steep Holm war. It would be remembered as being otherwise uneventful but in fact it was proving to be a vital achievement. What was happening, routinely and without disruption, in the waters beside the island, was changing the shape of the war in Europe.

Shipments into South Wales ports during 1941-44 would amount to the heaviest loads to be moved by water in the whole history of the world. They were the logistical support for the offensive war and would be crucial for the subsequent invasion of Europe.

End of the pier: seaward footings for that on Steep Holm, in the centre of the beach, with Rodney Legg inspecting. The rest of the structure has been removed. Seen from the west. Photographed by John Pitfield in 1990.

Concrete ridges, between Cliff Cottage and the Pump House: built late in 1941, to support iron water and diesel tanks. Water had to be imported from Barry after the island's Victorian reservoir became contaminated. From this point the water and diesel were pumped to the top of the island, to holding tanks on two similar grids of concrete on the southern edge of the the central plateau. Seen from the south (with warden Peter Rees on the right). Photographed by Colin Graham in 1974.

Searchlight post: one of the island's four anti-ship lights, facing north from the foot of
208 Steps midway along the precipitous side of the island. Built in 1941. Seen from the
sea, from the north. Photographed by Colin Graham in 1983.

**Searchlight post: anti-E boat precaution to enable the Steep Holm Coast Defence
Batteries to be operational at night. This one faces west from Rudder Rock. Built in
1941. Seen from the sea, from the south. Photographed by Colin Graham in 1983.**

Wartime zebra-camouflage: on the 1941-built searchlight post at Rudder Rock. Seen from the north-east. Painted by war artist Ray Howard Jones in 1943. Photographed by Stanley Rendell in 1978.

Searchlight post at Rudder Rock: showing the dramatic cliff-edge situation and the surviving monument to the efforts of the Royal Engineers in 1941. Seen from the north-east. Photographed by Rodney Legg in 1973.

Sans searchlight: empty interior of the Searchlight Post built in 1941 at the bottom of what is now known as 208 Steps (the figures having post-war significance as the frequency of Radio Luxembourg in the medium wave-

band). Seen from the south, looking seawards. Photographed by Colin Graham in 1983.

Flashback: searchlight similar to those installed on Steep Holm. Photographer unknown; probably on the south coast of England in 1940.

Off the rails: evidence of a mishap in October 1941, incised across the outer rail of the island's cliff railway near the top of the central incline. As the cradle of a six-inch gun was being winched up the track, one wheel of the truck slipped off and the weight dragged the other three wheels – gouging these scars (between the pebbles) as the whole load slipped down the cliff. Gunner Cyril Stickland recalls the incident, on page 85. Seen from the west. Photographed by Rodney Legg in 1991.

Waiting for the Germans: somewhere in southern England, in a concrete and girder position almost identical to that built by the Royal Engineers for the Battery Observation Post on Rudder Rock, in 1941.

Rudder Rock: the 1941-built Battery Observation Post (right) with a George III cannon muzzle (centre) and the remains of the tortoise-shaped armoured shield of the 1898 firings from HMS Arrogant (centre left). Seen from the south. Photographed by Colin Graham in 1975.

Precipice and bottom steps: concrete flight of stairs up from the Searchlight Post in the central northern cliffs. In places these are unsupported and rise through the air. The view is from the Searchlight Post at the foot of 208 Steps. Looking westwards, at low tide (hence seaweed-covered ledges exposed towards the lower right). Photographed by Colin Graham in 1983.

OVERLEAF, FIRST DOUBLE-PAGE SPREAD – **Western war-works: showing Palmerstonian Split Rock Battery (top centre), Summit Battery (centre left, with 1941-built Generator House and pair of 6-inch gun batteries), and Rudder Rock (lower right) with 1941 Battery Observation Post (on cliffs) and Searchlight Post (at the tip of the island). Seen from the north-west. Photographed by West Air Photography in 1976.**

SECOND DOUBLE-PAGE SPREAD – **Eastern war-works: showing the 1941-built pair of 6-inch gun batteries at Garden Battery West (centre, left) and Garden Battery East (centre, right). To the left of the first is a wartime Generator House. It supplied the two Searchlight Posts which are visible at South Landing (lower centre, on cliffs) and between Tower Rock and the offshore Calf Rock (lower mid-right). Note the tide race off these cliffs, which runs an hour after the tide has begun to ebb, over the beach and its shingle spit. It continues at this force for a couple of hours (the movement of the water in this picture is from top to bottom). Seen from the south-west. Photographed by Cambridge University in about 1955.**

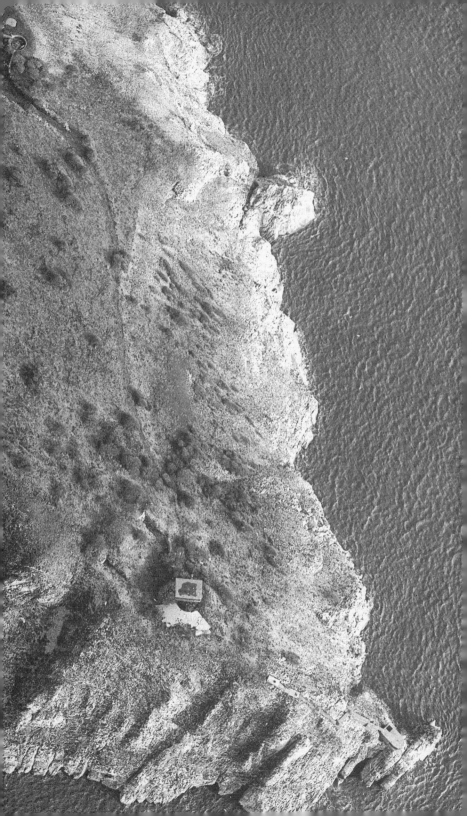

The first cargoes of lease-lend equipment from the United States of America were landed at Swansea in 1941. With the entry of the Americans into the war the South Wales ports were chosen for the import of all the massive volume of often exceedingly heavy equipment for the American forces. Just what these ships carried was on a scale that was betrayed by the derricks fixed to their decks. These could lift up to 120 tons at a time. The dockers called the special three-deck vessels the "Sea Trains" and they were indeed laid throughout with railway track and sometimes literally carried complete railway systems across the Atlantic.

When the SS *Lakehurst* waited the tide off Steep Holm in October 1943 she was preparing to unload 166 tanks and 16 other military vehicles at Newport. That cargo weighed a total of 4,285 tons. The *Lakehurst* appeared off the island again in December 1943, this time turning into Cardiff, and was then carrying 34 complete Austerity-class 2-8-0 railway locomotives. Cardiff became the largest supply dump in Europe and the docks that had been designed for the export of coal were used for the import of munitions. An additional yard was constructed with sidings that accommodated 1,500 wagons. Frozen meat was also coming across the Atlantic in immense quantities and the largest cold-storage depôt in Europe was built at Queen Alexandra Dock. Penarth docks, which had been closed in 1936, were re-opened and equipped with huge floating cranes to deal with the more ordinary cargoes.

It was a matter of some reassurance for sailors, dockers, and the people of the South Wales coast that the great offshore rock – which is a dominant backdrop to their daily lives – was bristling with friendly guns. Its war-works are now preserved, largely intact, as a memorial to their builders from the Royal Engineers and to the men of the Severn Fixed Defences. Their guns were a particularly welcome sight for the merchant seamen who had run the Atlantic gauntlet and had survived the U-boats and the treacherous South-Western Approaches. "Fortress Britain" began with Steep Holm.

In the 1980s there were still a stream of stories about the Steep Holm war years current in Weston-super-Mare. Perhaps the mainland stories came about because Steep Holm and Flat Holm were forbidden territory, an active part of the country's front line in the Battle of the Atlantic. Little real information filtered back to Weston as the islands were serviced from the Welsh side of the Channel.

It is Weston folklore that the two islands were virtually Britain's joint Alcatraz. Locals, as they tell you about the islands, give history a certain timeless quality by referring to both Steep Holm and Flat Holm individually in the plural. That is the way their names were written on Victorian maps.

Birnbeck Island, at the north end of Weston-super-Mare seafront, was the Admiralty's wartime Department of Miscellaneous Weapons Research and Development. Several of its creations were first tested in the waters off Steep Holm, including the ship-launched anti-submarine missile Amuck. This was a centrally-mounted Mark II depth charge containing 180 lb of high explosive and surrounded by twelve 2-inch diameter cordite rockets. These propelled it 500 yards but the range could be reduced, for closer targets, by removing opposite pairs of rockets.

The initial trials were from a ramp at the tip of Brean Down, which has a rail and points almost directly at Steep Holm. Its shallow elevation is about ten degrees above horizontal. Amuck went into Royal Navy use as a transversable angle-iron and steel launching structure which was initially mounted near the bows but later provided with a rotating base to give wider scope for the positioning.

Another Miscellaneous Weapons Department project, also developed at the HMS Birnbeck shore-base, is mentioned in the National Trust booklet on *Brean Down*. This was a rocket-launched Expendable Noisemaker which became a ship-towed decoy to lure German submarines and acoustic torpedoes from their intended target. The story in this booklet of one of the missiles taking off from Brean Down and ending up in a farm-yard is a complete myth, as John Pitfield points out: "Details of an erratic flight probably have some truth, but an account of a stray missile going inland are pure fiction, because of the weapon's short range and the position of the launch-rail. The account in the booklet suggests that the weapon was unsuccessful, but all available information is that these were the initial trials and trouble-shooting phase."

Development was transferred to the Shoeburyness ranges in the Thames estuary. The Expendable Noisemaker was then put into production.

John Watts is the Weston boatman who runs the Steep Holm ferry and he cherishes tales of both islands' past: "In the last war both islands, Steep Holms and Flat Holms, were used by the army. Flat Holms was an experimental place, especially for developing radar, because no one could hear or see what was happening. The place had 600 men and today most of the buildings are still there, vandalised, including rows of lavatories. German prisoners were also kept on Flat Holms – they were not the ordinary ones, but twelve desperate and dangerous Germans, and they were kept in barred cells. It's not the sort of place you can escape from, but one batch tried it on logs or something and were caught up the Channel at the English and Welsh Grounds Lightship. Another group, of two I think also tried it, but were drowned. Some of these prisoners were taken over to Steep Holms for work parties.''

To his regret, Major Benger had to consign most of that account to legend. Yes, Flat Holm was far more intensively used, and more heavily armed, to give flak-cover for Cardiff, but the maximum complement was 350 servicemen. By the time the German prisoners arrived at Flat Holm they no longer had any reason to be desperate or dangerous. Major Benger used them to clear up the island at the end of the war: ''The German prisoners were out there to dismantle the fortifications, not to be imprisoned. There are no barred cells, or any places at all where men could be detained, and such men would have been the very last to be chosen if they needed tight supervision and control.'' The confusion had arisen because a huge prisoner-of-war camp was at Island Farm, which was not at sea at all but lies on the South Wales mainland, between Porthcawl and Bridgend. It was from there that a large number of German officers tunnelled to temporary freedom in the middle of the war, but that, as they say, is another story.

Royal Navy Isle-class trawler HMS Steepholm: 'DV 17' seen above and opposite in her post-war wreck-dispersal role. She worked in the Thames Estuary and the North Sea. Photographer unknown; probably at Great Yarmouth in 1953.

HMS Steepholm

The island's name was carried during the war by HMS *Steepholm*. She was one of the numerous "Isle"-class armed trawlers built for the Royal Navy during the Second World War for anti-submarine and minesweeping purposes. They were the largest class of Admiralty-designed dual purpose trawlers with 130 being constructed in the United Kingdom between 1941-45 and others built in Canadian and Indian yards.

HMS *Steepholm* was of 545 tons displacement. Ordered in 1942, she was laid down at the Aberdeen shipyard of John Lewis Limited, in April 1943. Launched on 15 July 1943, she was provided with one 12-pounder and three 20 mm anti-aircraft guns, and 30 depth-charges. On 1 December 1943 she was commissioned for service.

As "DV 17" *Steepholm* was attached to the Nore Command in the Thames Estuary. After the war her weapons were taken off and she was equipped with a crane and chains as a Wreck Dispersal Vessel. She was based at Sheerness and continued working there, clearing wartime wrecks and redundant offshore defences, until October 1958. In June 1960 she was sold for scrap.

The crash of the Javelin

Her sister ship *Flatholm* had much closer associations with the island, culminating in the biggest ever search of the waters around Steep Holm, which began on 21 October 1954 and went on for several weeks. Flight Lieutenant R.J. Ross of the Royal Air Force went down in one of Britain's newest jet aircraft, the large and distinctively shaped delta-wing and delta-tail Gloster Javelin interceptor fighter.

Ross was posted "missing, presumed killed". The surface fleet that looked for the remains of the aeroplane totalled ten vessels. Their principal area of operation was between Steep Holm and Weston Bay.

Commander T.D. Butler, the Boom Defence Officer from Pembroke Dock, South Wales, co-ordinated the effort from his own craft, *Barrage*. He also had the use of the frigate *Venus*, the minesweeping trawler *Flatholm*, the minesweepers *Chillingham* and *Asheldham*, three seaward defence craft, and two tugs.

Zero underwater visibility ruled out the use of television cameras suspended on cables. Instead the operation relied upon sweep wires which sometimes came up with paint-marks from contact with pieces of the aircraft but in mid-November the Admiralty announced that "it has not been possible to establish the exact position of the contacts".

By this time the sweeping had been abandoned and only HMS *Flatholm* remained off the island. She acted as the parent ship for teams of divers.

Because of the tide race, they could only work in the half-hour slot of slack water as the tide changed, and complained that the conditions were the worst they had ever worked in. The turbidity meant that everything had to be sensed by feel alone. For a time the weather co-operated, but luck did not.

Javelins were meanwhile released from their grounding and cleared for flight, but the cause of the Steep Holm crash was never established. Or at least, there was no public explanation regarding the sensitive loss with its pilot of a newly-introduced front-line combat aircraft

Warplane aerobatics

Military aircraft have continued to be regular users of the Bristol Channel, from the Royal Air Force and the Royal Navy, along with test pilots of the British Aircraft Corporation, now British Aerospace, from their main factory at Filton. At times these have become more than matters of training and testing.

RAF Transport Command from Lyneham, Wiltshire, has been the regular user of the Bristol Channel flight-path when the world edges towards war. In 1956-57 the general workhorse was the four-engined Hastings, supplemented by two-engined turbo-prop Britannias and the first jet airliners, Mark II Comets. Their next stop, for refuelling, was Gibraltar, and crisis destinations such as Suez and the EOKA uprising in Cyprus.

The years of decolonisation were marked by a series of conflicts, leading to the great air armada of 1982 when the Empire struck back, with Ascension Island as the staging post and for a few stressful months the world's busiest airport, leading to the retaking of the Falkland Islands.

That summer of the winter war in the South Atlantic, Chris Maslen and Jenny Smith were living on the island, working on the Barracks roof as the shuttle-service of four-engined C130 Lockheed Hercules transports lumbered heavily outward-bound down the Bristol Channel, enabling them to look down on the wing panels and start to count the bolt-heads.

The same aircraft were back, though in lesser numbers, for the crisis in the Persian Gulf in 1990, en route this time for Gibraltar. One visitor remarked to me upon a Hercules that was flying close to the water, down-Channel, at the August bank holiday. "Must be going to an air show," he observed.

"Some air day!" I interjected. "He's going to war."

"Oh of course," the man replied.

Half an hour later another Hercules came from the opposite direction, the west, but this time as an empty high-flying speck, at 5,000 feet, on a gradual descent inward from the open sea towards Marlborough Downs.

During the forty-three days of war in the Gulf, in January and February 1991, the Bristol Channel was selected as the least risky route of return for any damaged American B52 heavy bombers returning from active service to their temporary war-base at Fairford on the eastern side of the Cotswolds. Had they still been carrying bombs, these were to have been dumped – though not primed to explode – in the extensive sea danger area that begins ten kilometres off Hartland Point and extends in a great arc from fifty kilometres south-west to fifty kilometres north-north-east. It includes Lundy Island. Danger area D116/20 is controlled by Chivenor Approach on 130.2 MHz or London Military via 124.75 MHz.

Much closer to Steep Holm, though nothing like the size of the Lundy danger area, is bombing range D119/5 in the southern part of Bridgwater Bay, westwards from Hinkley Point to Watchet. This is controlled by Yeovilton Approach on 127.35 MHz.

At night the extremities of this danger area are clearly visible from Steep Holm; being the lights of Hinkley Point nuclear power station in the east and to the west the column of red lights on the 508-feet tower at Williton that is a GCHQ listening-post, operating as an out-station of the Government Communications Headquarters, which is based in Cheltenham.

Aerial activity in the Bristol Channel was much diminished in the winter of 1990-91 when the front-line Tornado fighter-bombers departed for the Persian Gulf. With them went most of the Royal Navy's Sea King helicopters. The peacetime land-base for the latter is at Yeovilton, which has its Area of Intense Aerial Activity across the Somerset Levels and extending sea-wards to a point six kilometres south of Steep Holm.

Those Tornadoes – or Tornados, the preferred spelling when they became daily news, carrying out daring and costly low-level attacks on Iraqi airfields and bridges – provide the most exhilarating air displays imaginable. Steep Holm is a superb platform for viewing their breathtaking manoeuvrability, though it is a restricted show as the RAF generally performs only on weekdays.

The best attack runs are when a section of two aircraft comes westwards from the open sea and splits, sometimes crossing in an 'X' as they approach Rudder Rock, and then fly at half the height of the island along the north and south sides. They emerge from behind Tower Rock and Laboratory Battery at about a hundred feet and then frequently re-cross the 'X' as they proceed up to the Severn Bridge.

Though bombless and subsonic they are still potentially menacing and very fast; indeed their speed is too fast for the sound and if you follow your ears you will miss them. I once saw a single Tornado – a lone combat aircraft is the flying prerogative of a Squadron Leader – go low up-Channel towards Clevedon and then suddenly rise from the horizontal into a vertical climb which took it up like a rocket to become a speck in the atmosphere, beyond 25,000 feet.

On the other end of the scale, the closest near-miss I have seen was when a Tornado streaked from west to east beside the Barracks at island-height as a small civilian helicopter came from behind the north side of the island and emerged beside Tower Rock. The Tornado banked leftwards and upwards to zoom above it; I wondered if either pilot would report the incident and somehow doubted it.

That first layer of air-space belongs to the military. Above, from 1,000 to 3,000 feet altitude, it is the north-east corner of the Cardiff Special Rules Area for civilian aircraft descending towards Cardiff Aerodrome, controlled by Cardiff Approach on 125.85 MHz.

The closest fly-past we witnessed by a civilian aeroplane took place on a misty winter evening in 1989-90 when an airliner approached the Barracks from the east. The intensity of sound was such that Steven Murdoch and I ran outside the building. The ground was illuminated by the landing lights of an Airbus which was hardly a hairline crack above 80 feet as it skimmed the top of the island. I shone my torch along the length of the fuselage at faces staring in disbelief from the long line of portholes.

This close-encounter was followed by a slow turn northwards, for what little remained of the descent into Cardiff. Nothing more was heard, either literally or later, as fate intervened once again to keep us from the News at Ten.

Plastic armour: invented in 1940, with Steep Holm one of its first users, in October 1941. It would save the Allies millions of tons of steel during the course of World War II. Specimen from Garden Battery East (from a metre-square slab of 70 mm thickness). Photographed by Barry Cousens in 1991.

INDEX